Fat Quarter Quilts™

Edited by Jeanne Stauffer & Sandra L. Hatch

HOUSE of
WHITE
BIRCHES

PUBLISHERS
SINCE 1947

Fat Quarter Quilts

Editors: Jeanne Stauffer and Sandra L. Hatch
Associate Editor: Dianne Schmidt
Design Associate: Vicki Blizzard
Book and Cover Design: Jessi Butler
Copy Editors: Sue Harvey, Nicki Lehman, Mary Martin
Publications Coordinator: Tanya Turner

Photography: Jeff Chilcote, Tammy Christian,
Kelly Heydinger, Nancy Sharp
Photography Assistant: Linda Quinlan

Publishing Services Manager: Brenda Gallmeyer
Technical Artist: Connie Rand
Graphic Artist: Ronda Bechinski, Kristen Sprunger
Production Assistants: Janet Bowers, Marj Morgan
Traffic Coordinator: Sandra Beres

Publishers: Carl H. Muselman, Arthur K. Muselman
Chief Executive Officer: John Robinson
Publishing Marketing Director: David McKee
Book Marketing Manager: Craig Scott
Product Development Director: Vivian Rothe
Publishing Services Director: Brenda R. Wendling

Printed in the United States of America
First Printing: 2002
Library of Congress Number: 2001097994
ISBN: 1-882138-93-7

A Quick Note

Isn't it fun to buy fat quarters! One of the first things we look for when we enter a quilt shop is its display of fat quarters. Some shops have them all folded nice and neat—a small stack of coordinated fabrics tied with a ribbon and ready to be used in a project.

Other shops have boxes of them folded and lined up with all the fabrics of a similar color in one place. These boxes always look like a rainbow of fabric and color. These displays make it easy to select fabrics for a project when you want a small amount of a variety of fabrics in a certain color.

We love displays that fill lunch boxes or miniature crates with fat quarters or that make the fat quarters look like a giant lollipop. There are so many creative ways to display fat quarters! Likewise, there are so many creative ways to use fat quarters to make full-size quilts and smaller projects. That is what we share with you in this book!

If you are like us, whenever you visit a quilt shop or fabric store, fat quarters just seem to call your name and say, "Take me home with you." We have included in this collection a wide variety of quilts and projects made from fat quarters, including several borders for large quilts.

If you love to buy fat quarters, you will love the projects in this book. All those fabric treasures you have found in fat quarter displays can now find a home in a project used to decorate your home or to give as a gift to someone you love.

We wish you hours of happy fat quarter quilting!

Warmly,

Jeanne Stauffer

Sandra L. Hatch

Contents

Babytime Quilts

Teddy-Go-Round 8

Sleepy Baby Buggy 11

Happy Penguins...15

Teddy Bear Quilt & Tote 18

Celebration 23

Baby Blocks With Love............................27

Christmas Keepsakes

Checkerboard Four-Patch 32

Nativity Wall Quilt....................................35

Christmas Cardinal 40

Sign of the Season 46

Flaky Friends 50

Christmas Keepsake Stocking 54

One-Color Quilting

By the Seashore...60

Hearts Afloat 63

Blue Floral Lap Quilt................................66

Sunny Days 71

Golden Pansies Table Mat 74

Blue for You Kimono................................78

Fat Quarter Classics

Evergreen Lane 86

Dragonfly Meadow 90

Hearts United...............................93

Stars & Stripes Table Quilt 96

United We Stand 100

Maple Leaf Ragtime 103

Pretty Maids 106

3-D Quilting

Ruched Roses & Baskets 112

Posey Patch................................116

Flowers & Grapes Baskets.........119

The Earth Laughs in Flowers.....123

Gather Ye Roses.........................130

Petals & Leaves Pillow 136

Appliqué for Fun

Spring Bouquets 142

Oriental Garden 150

Flower Basket Mantel Cover 155

Homespun Pumpkin Patch Vest...............159

Posy Silhouettes.........................162

Flowers at the Crossroads 165

General Instructions 170

Special Thanks 176

Fabrics & Supplies 176

Babytime Quilts

Colorful teddy bears, penguins, hearts and baby buggies are stitched from fat quarters to lovingly create quilts, throws and totes for your precious little ones.

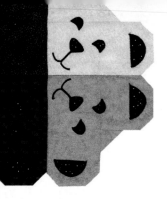

Teddy-Go-Round

By Sue Harvey

Make a play-on-the-floor quilt for a small child who will be happy to have friendly teddies peering up at him.

Project Specifications

Skill Level: Beginner

Quilt Size: 44 1/2" x 44 1/2"

Block Size: 12" x 12"

Number of Blocks: 9

Bear's Fancy
12" x 12" Block

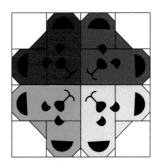

Teddy-Go-Round
12" x 12" Block

Materials

- 4 bright-colored print fat quarters
- 1 black print fat quarter
- 3/4 yard white print
- 1 1/2 yards bear print
- Batting 49" x 49"
- Backing 49" x 49"
- All-purpose thread to match fabrics
- Black machine-embroidery thread
- 1/4 yard fusible transfer web
- 1 yard fabric stabilizer
- Basting spray
- Basic sewing tools and supplies, rotary cutter, mat and ruler, and marking pencil

Instructions

Note: Fabrics will be referred to as bright, black, white or bear throughout these instructions.

Step 1. Cut two strips 4 3/4" x 36 1/2" across width of bear print; cut two strips 4 3/4" x 36 1/2" along length of bear print. Set aside for borders. *Note: For a non-directional print, cut all four strips across the width of the fabric.*

Step 2. Cut four squares bear print 5 1/2" x 5 1/2" for K. *Note: For a directional print, cut on the fabric diagonal to keep print upright in blocks.*

Step 3. Cut three strips white print 1 1/4" by fabric width; subcut each strip into 1 1/4" square segments for C. You will need 80 C squares.

Step 4. Cut two strips white print 3 1/2" by fabric width; subcut each strip into 3 1/2" square segments for D. You will need 20 D squares.

Step 5. Cut one strip white print 4 3/8" by fabric width; subcut into 4 3/8" square segments. Cut each square on one diagonal to make H triangles; you will need 16 H triangles.

Step 6. Cut one strip white print 6 1/4" by fabric width; subcut into 6 1/4" square segments. Cut each square on both diagonals to make J triangles; you will need 16 J triangles.

Step 7. From each bright fat quarter, cut the following strips: one 6 1/2" x 18"—subcut into five 3 1/2" segments for A; one 3 1/2" x 18"—subcut into five 3 1/2" squares for B; one 1 3/4" x 18"—subcut into five 1 3/4" squares for E and one 5 1/2" x 18" —subcut into four 4" segments for G.

Step 8. Mark a diagonal line from corner to corner on the wrong side of each C and E square.

Step 9. To piece one teddy unit, place a C square right sides together on two adjacent corners of A as shown in Figure 1; stitch on the marked line, trim seam allowance to 1/4" and press C open as shown in Figure 2. Repeat on a same-color B as shown in Figure 3.

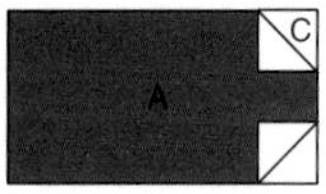

Figure 1
Place C on 2 adjacent corners of A.

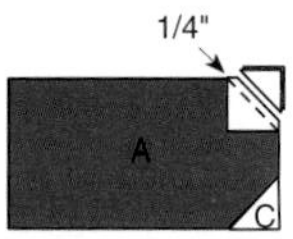

Figure 2
Stitch, trim and press C open.

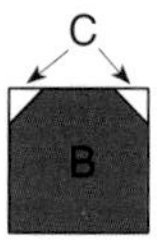

Figure 3
Complete 1 B-C unit as shown.

Step 10. Place a same-color E on one corner of D; stitch, trim and press E open as shown in Figure 4.

Figure 4
Complete 1 D-E unit as shown.

Step 11. Sew B-C to D-E as shown in

Figure 5; add A-C to complete one teddy unit, again referring to Figure 5. Repeat to make five teddy units of each color.

Step 12. Trace large teddy eye, ear and nose pieces on the paper side of the fusible transfer web referring to the patterns for number to trace of each; fuse to the wrong side of the black print.

Figure 5
Complete 1 teddy unit as shown.

Step 13. Cut out each piece on the traced line; remove paper backing.

Step 14. Fuse one nose, two eye and two ear pieces to each teddy unit referring to the block drawing for positioning; mark the mouth shape given below each nose piece. Pin a piece of fabric stabilizer on the wrong side of each teddy unit.

Step 15. Using black machine-embroidery thread in the top of the machine and all-purpose thread in the bobbin and a medium-width zigzag stitch, machine-stitch around each fused shape and along the marked mouth lines; remove fabric stabilizer.

Step 16. Join one teddy unit of each color to complete one Teddy-Go-Round block referring to the block drawing for positioning of units; repeat for five blocks.

Step 17. To piece one Bear's Fancy block, sew J to opposite ends of one bright G as shown in Figure 6; add H to one long side, again referring to Figure 6. Repeat with different-color G.

Figure 6
Sew J to opposite ends of G; add H.

Figure 7
Sew G to opposite sides of K; add H.

Step 18. Sew a G of the remaining two colors to opposite sides of K as shown in Figure 7; add H to the G ends of the pieced unit, again referring to Figure 7.

Step 19. Join the pieced units to complete one Bear's Fancy block referring to the block drawing for positioning; repeat for four blocks.

Step 20. Join the blocks in three rows of three blocks each as shown in Figure 8; join the rows to complete the pieced center.

Step 21. From each bright fat quarter, cut the following: one 2" x 18" strip—subcut into one

Make 1

Make 2

Figure 8
Join the blocks in rows of 3 blocks each.

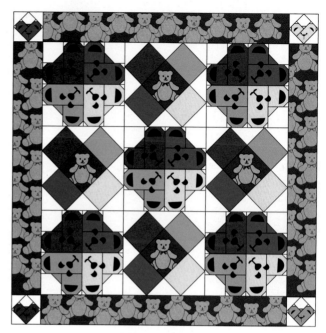

Teddy-Go-Round
Placement Diagram
44 1/2" x 44 1/2"

3 1/2" segment for A, one 2" square for B and one 1 1/4" x 1 1/4" square for E.

Step 22. From white print, cut the following: 16 squares 7/8" x 7/8" for C, four squares 2" x 2" for D and eight squares 3" x 3" for F. Cut each F square in half on one diagonal to make 16 F triangles.

Step 23. Piece one small teddy unit of each color referring to steps 8–11. Sew an F triangle to each side of the teddy units to complete a corner unit.

Step 24. Mark the small teddy mouth, nose, eye and ear shapes on each unit using the pattern given; pin a piece of fabric stabilizer on the wrong side of each corner unit.

Step 25. Using black machine-embroidery thread in the top of the machine and all-purpose thread in the bobbin, machine satin-stitch each shape; remove fabric stabilizer.

Step 26. Sew a fabric-length strip cut in Step 1 to opposite sides of the pieced center; press seams toward strips.

Step 27. Sew a corner unit to opposite ends of each remaining bear print strip; sew a strip to the top and bottom of the pieced center to complete the top. Press seams toward strips.

Step 28. Apply basting spray to one side of the batting piece; place on the wrong side of the prepared backing piece. Repeat with completed top.

Continued on page 26

Sleepy Baby Buggy

By Marian Shenk

*Whether your special baby is a girl or a boy, this crib blanket
is a perfect fit for nice walks with a baby carriage.*

Project Notes

Buttons and bows may be eliminated for children old enough to possibly pick them off and create a choking hazard.

Project Specifications

Skill Level: Beginner

Quilt Size: 31 1/2" x 46 1/2"

Block Size: 7 1/2" x 9"

Number of Blocks: 12

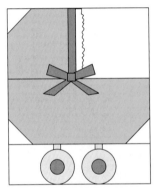

Pink Buggy
7 1/2" x 9" Block

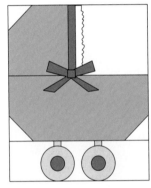

Blue Buggy
7 1/2" x 9" Block

Materials

- 2 fat quarters each light pink and light blue prints
- 2 fat quarters each dark pink and dark blue prints
- 3 fat quarters each cream-on-cream prints or 3/4 yard
- Batting 35" x 50"
- Backing 35" x 50"
- All-purpose thread to match fabrics
- Cream hand-quilting thread
- 1 yard 1/2"-wide white lace
- 6 each 1/2" blue and pink buttons
- 1 1/8 yards each 3/8"-wide blue and pink satin ribbon

Nine-Patch
7 1/2" x 9" Block

- 2 packages blue wide bias binding
- Basic sewing tools and supplies, rotary cutter, mat and ruler, and marking pencil

Instructions

Step 1. Cut two strips 4 1/4" x 22" cream-on-cream print; subcut each strip into 4" segments for A. You will need six cream-on-cream print A pieces.

Step 2. Cut three 4" x 4 1/4" rectangles each light pink and light blue prints for A.

Step 3. Cut three 4" x 8" rectangles each light pink and light blue prints for C.

Step 4. Cut six 2 1/2" x 8" rectangles cream-on-cream print for D.

Step 5. Prepare templates for wheel and axle pieces using patterns given; cut as directed on each piece, adding a 1/4" seam allowance all around for hand appliqué. Turn under seam allowance all around on each piece. Place axel pieces, then wheel pieces on D as shown in Figure 1 for positioning. Hand-appliqué in place on all D pieces.

Figure 1
Place wheel pieces,
ending with circle on D.

Step 6. Cut two strips 1 3/4" x 22" cream-on-cream print; subcut each strip into 1 3/4" squares for B; you will need 18 B squares. Draw a diagonal line from corner to corner on the wrong side of each B square.

Step 7. Place one B square on the corner of a light blue print A square referring to Figure 2 for positioning of square. Stitch on the marked line; trim seam to 1/4" and press B to the right side as shown in Figure 3. Repeat on all light blue and light pink print A pieces.

Figure 2
Place 1 B square on
the corner of a light
blue print A square.

Figure 3
Stitch on the marked line;
trim seam to 1/4" and
press B to the right side.

Step 8. Place one B square on two corners of a light blue print C piece referring to Figure 4 for positioning of squares. Stitch on the marked line; trim seam to 1/4" and press B to the right side as shown in Figure 5. Repeat on all light blue and light pink print C pieces.

Figure 4
Place 1 B square on
2 corners of a light
blue print C piece.

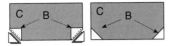

Figure 5
Stitch on the marked line;
trim seam to 1/4" and
press B to the right side.

Step 9. Cut six 4" lengths 1/2"-wide white lace; baste to one 4" side of each cream-on-cream print A piece.

Step 10. To piece one Blue Buggy block, sew a cream-on-cream print/lace A to a light blue print A-B unit as shown in Figure 6.

Figure 6
Sew a cream-on-cream
print/lace A to a light blue
print A-B unit.

Step 11. Cut three 4" lengths each 3/8"-wide pink and blue satin ribbon. Topstitch a matching color ribbon piece over seam between the A-lace units as shown in Figure 7.

Figure 7
Topstitch a matching color
ribbon piece over seam
between the A-lace units.

Step 12. Add C and D units to a matching color A unit referring to Figure 8. Repeat for three Blue Buggy and three Pink Buggy blocks. Press seams toward darker fabrics.

Figure 8
Add C and D to a
matching color A unit.

Step 13. Cut two strips light blue print, three strips light pink print and four strips cream-on-cream print 3 1/2" x 22"; subcut each strip into 3" segments for E. You will need 12 light blue print, 18 light pink print and 24 cream-on-cream print E pieces.

Step 14. Arrange the E pieces in rows referring to Figure 9. Join pieces in rows; join rows to complete one Nine-Patch block. Repeat for six Nine-Patch blocks; press seams in one direction.

Figure 9
Arrange the E
pieces in rows.

Step 15. Cut nine rectangles each 2" x 9 1/2" dark blue and dark pink prints for F.

Step 16. Join blocks and F pieces to make rows as shown in Figure 10.

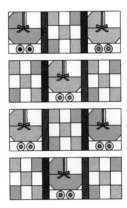

Figure 10
Join blocks and F
pieces to make rows.

Step 17. Cut two rectangles each dark blue and dark pink prints 2" x 8" for G.

Step 18. Join F and G pieces to make sashing rows referring to Figure 11; press seams in one direction.

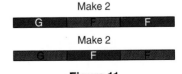

Figure 11
Join F and G pieces to
make sashing rows.

Step 19. Join the pieced rows with the F-G sashing rows as shown in Figure 12; press seams toward sashing rows.

Step 20. Cut four rectangles dark blue print and five rectangles dark pink print 2" x 11" for H. Join two of each color H pieces to make a side border strip as shown in Figure 13; repeat for two strips. Sew a strip to opposite sides of the pieced center; press seams toward strips.

Figure 12
Join the pieced rows with the F-G sashing rows.

Figure 13
Join 2 of each color H pieces to make a side border strip.

Step 21. Join the remaining two F pieces with the remaining H piece to make the top sashing row as shown in Figure 14; sew to the top edge of the pieced center. Press seams toward strip.

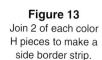

Figure 14
Join the remaining 2 F pieces with the remaining H piece to make the top sashing row.

Step 22. Cut (and piece) two strips each 2" x 32" and 2" x 44" cream-on-cream print. Sew the longer strips to opposite sides and shorter strips to the top and bottom of the pieced center; press seams toward strips.

Step 23. Prepare top for quilting, quilt and bind edges using purchased blue wide bias binding referring to the General Instructions. *Note: The quilt shown was hand-quilted in the ditch of seams and around wheel shapes using cream hand-quilting thread.*

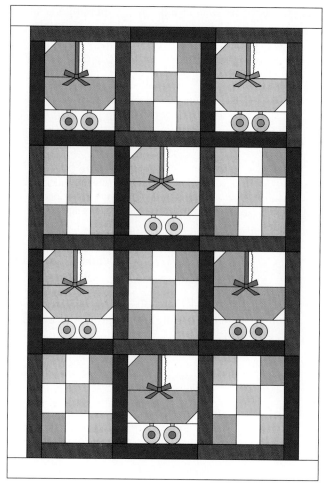

Sleepy Baby Buggy
Placement Diagram
31 1/2" x 46 1/2"

Step 24. Sew a matching color button in the center of each appliquéd wheel.

Step 25. Cut three 9" lengths each 3/8"-wide pink and blue satin ribbon. Tie each length to make a bow; hand-stitch a bow at the base of each A/ribbon/lace unit to finish. ❖

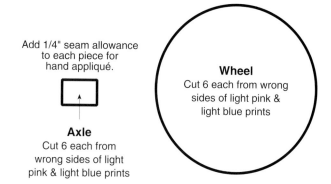

Add 1/4" seam allowance to each piece for hand appliqué.

Axle
Cut 6 each from wrong sides of light pink & light blue prints

Wheel
Cut 6 each from wrong sides of light pink & light blue prints

Happy Penguins

By Kate Laucomer

This cold-weather quilt will have your child counting penguins instead of sheep at nap time or bedtime.

Project Note

If this quilt will be made for a very small child, eliminate button eyes for safety reasons. Make satin-stitched eyes using white embroidery floss with a black French knot in the center.

Project Specifications

Skill Level: Beginner

Quilt Size: 44 1/2" x 52 1/2"

Block Size: 9" x 11"

Number of Blocks: 16

Materials

- 4" x 8" scrap gold mottled
- 1 fat quarter each 4 different red prints
- 1 fat quarter each 6 or 7 different white-on-white prints
- 1 fat quarter each 6 or 7 different black-and-white prints
- 1 1/2 yards red print for border and binding
- Batting 49" x 57"
- Backing 49" x 57"
- All-purpose thread to match fabrics
- Black machine-embroidery thread
- Red and white machine-quilting thread
- 1 1/2 yards fusible transfer web
- 3/4 yard fabric stabilizer
- 16 (1/4") white buttons
- Basic sewing tools and supplies, rotary cutter, mat and ruler, and white paper

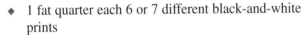

Penguin
9" x 11" Block

Instructions

Step 1. Cut four rectangles 7 1/2" x 9 1/2" from each red print fat quarter for background.

Step 2. Cut five 2" x 22" (A) strips and sixteen 1 1/2" x 22" (B) strips along the length of the white-on-white print fat quarters. *Note: Be sure to leave large enough pieces to cut appliqué pieces later.* Repeat with black-and-white prints to make A and B strips.

Step 3. Trace the penguin pattern onto a piece of white paper with a dark pen or marker. Place fusible transfer web with paper side up on top of pattern and trace eight of each penguin part onto the paper. Turn pattern over and trace eight of each part reversed.

Step 4. Cut out traced shapes, leaving a small margin around each one. Fuse the stomach shapes to the wrong side of the white-on-white print fat quarters and the back, feet and flipper shapes on the wrong side of the black-and-white prints. Fuse the beak pieces to the wrong side of the gold mottled.

Step 5. Cut out shapes on traced lines; remove paper backing.

Step 6. Position one penguin motif on a red print background rectangle with head approximately 2" from top edge and tip of tail approximately 1 5/8" from side edge referring to Figure 1. Fuse in place in numerical order referring to pattern. Repeat for 16 blocks.

Figure 1
Fuse pieces in place as shown.

Step 7. Cut sixteen 5" x 7" rectangles fabric stabilizer; pin one rectangle to the wrong side of each fused block.

Step 8. Using black machine-embroidery thread in the top of the machine and all-purpose thread in the bobbin, machine blanket-stitch around each shape. When stitching is complete, remove fabric stabilizer.

Step 9. Cut one 9 1/2" strip from each white-on-white print B strip. Sew one strip to the right edge of each block as shown in Figure 2; press seams toward strips.

Figure 2
Sew strips to block as shown.

Step 10. Cut one 8 1/2" strip from each white-on-white print B strip; sew a strip to the bottom of each block, again referring to Figure 2. Press seams toward strips.

Step 11. Cut one 10 1/2" strip from each black-and-white print B strip. Sew a strip to the left edge of each block as shown in Figure 3; press seams toward strips.

Step 12. Cut one 9 1/2" strip from remainder of the black-and-white print B strips. Sew a strip to the top of each block, again referring to Figure 3; press seams toward strips to complete the Penguin blocks.

Step 13. Arrange blocks in four rows of four blocks each referring to the Placement Diagram for positioning of blocks. *Note: You may arrange the blocks with penguins dancing in any direction. Be sure to lay the blocks out and view before sewing together in rows.*

Step 14. Join the blocks in rows; join rows to complete the quilt center. Press seams in one direction.

Step 15. Join white-on-white print A strips on short ends to make one long strip. Repeat with black-and-white print A strips.

Step 16. Cut one 44 1/2" strip and one 38" strip from the black-and-white print A strip. Sew the longer strip to the right edge of the quilt center; press seam toward strip. Sew the shorter strip to the bottom edge of the quilt center; press seam toward strip.

Step 17. Cut one 46" strip and one 39 1/2" strip from the white-on-white print A strip. Sew the longer strip to the left edge of the quilt center; press seam toward strip. Sew the shorter strip to the top edge of the quilt center; press seam toward strip.

Step 18. Cut two strips each 3 1/4" x 45" and 3 1/4" x 47 1/2" along length of the red print. Sew the longer strips to opposite long sides and shorter strips to the top and bottom of the quilt center; press seams toward strips.

Step 19. Prepare quilt for quilting referring to the General Instructions. *Note: The sample quilt was machine-quilted using machine-quilting thread to match fabrics.*

Step 20. Prepare 6 yards self-made binding from red print and apply referring to the General Instructions.

Step 21. Sew a 1/4" white button to each penguin as marked on pat-

Figure 3
Sew strips to block as shown.

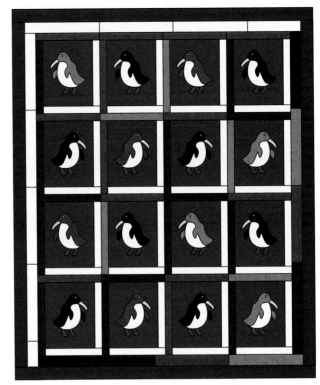

Happy Penguins
Placement Diagram
44 1/2" x 52 1/2"

tern for eye. ❖

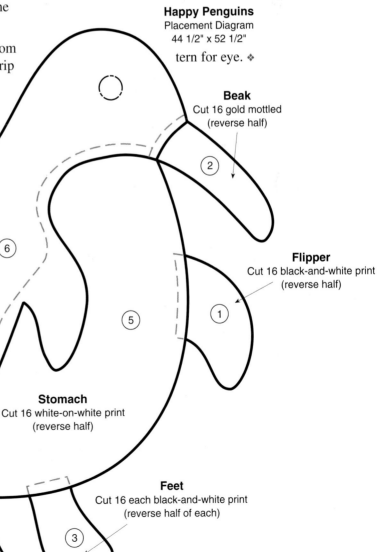

Beak
Cut 16 gold mottled
(reverse half)

Flipper
Cut 16 black-and-white print
(reverse half)

Back
Cut 16 black-and-white print
(reverse half)

Stomach
Cut 16 white-on-white print
(reverse half)

Feet
Cut 16 each black-and-white print
(reverse half of each)

Babytime Quilts **17**

Teddy Bear Quilt & Tote

By Pearl Louise Krush

Make this fringed baby quilt with matching tote using soft flannels or homespuns.

Project Note

The quilt will fold up and fit nicely inside the tote bag for easy transportation.

Teddy Bear Quilt

Project Specifications

Skill Level: Beginner

Quilt Size: 32" x 32"

Materials

- 6" x 6" piece brown felt
- 8 fat quarters different plaids or prints of homespun or flannel
- 1 fat quarter light brown flannel
- 1 yard cotton batting
- 1 1/4 yards backing flannel or homespun
- All-purpose thread to match fabrics
- Light brown 6-strand embroidery floss
- Basic sewing tools and supplies, embroidery needle, rotary cutter, mat and ruler, and water-erasable marker or pencil

Instructions

Step 1. Cut two 10" x 10" squares from each plaid or print homespun or flannel fat quarter.

Step 2. Cut sixteen 10" x 10" squares from backing flannel or homespun.

Step 3. Cut sixteen 8" x 8" squares cotton batting.

Step 4. Center and sandwich an 8" x 8" square of batting between a 10" x 10" square of plaid or homespun and a backing square.

Step 5. Using a water-erasable marker or pencil, draw diagonal lines from corner to corner of each layered square to make an X starting 1" from edge as shown in Figure 1.

Figure 1
Draw diagonal lines from corner to corner to make an X starting 1" from edge.

Step 6. Stitch on marked lines on each layered unit, securing beginning and ending stitches.

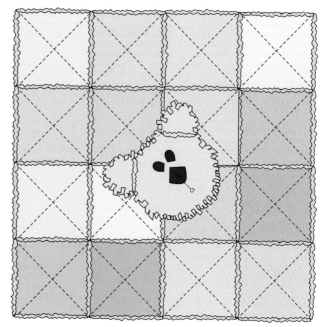

Teddy Bear Quilt
Placement Diagram
32" x 32"

Step 7. Arrange the squares in rows of four squares each, positioning squares with colors in a pleasing arrangement.

Step 8. Join the squares in rows with wrong sides together using a 1" seam allowance as shown in Figure 2; repeat for four rows. Press flat on the wrong side.

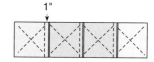

Figure 2
Join the squares in rows with wrong sides together using a 1" seam.

Step 9. Join rows with wrong sides together using a 1" seam; press flat on the wrong side. *Note: The raw seam allowances will be on the right side of the quilt.*

Step 10. Prepare patterns for large bear pieces using patterns given; cut as directed on each piece.

Step 11. Layer two ear pieces with wrong sides together; stitch around curved sides using a 1/2" seam allowance. Sew the ears to two top angled edges of the head piece with wrong sides together using a 1/2" seam allowance.

Step 12. Center and pin the head/ear shape to the stitched quilt top referring to the Placement Diagram

for positioning; mark around outside of shapes on quilt using the water-erasable marker or pencil. Remove head/ear shape; trim seam allowances of seams inside traced shape to 1/8".

Step 13. Pin the head/ear shape in place again; sew to the quilt top 1/2" from edge of shapes.

Step 14. Stitch around outside of quilt 1" from edge. Clip the outer edge and each seam to within 1/8" of the stitched line every scant 1/4". Repeat on head/ear shape seams and outer edge.

Step 15. Wash and dry the quilt to make edges fringe; remove all loose threads.

Step 16. Using 2 strands of brown embroidery floss, blanket-stitch the eyes and nose in place on the head/ear shape. Chain-stitch a mouth using drawing given to finish.

Teddy Bear Tote

Project Specifications

Skill Level: Beginner

Tote Size: 8" x 8" x 2"

Materials

- Scrap brown felt
- 1 fat quarter multicolor plaid homespun or flannel
- 1 fat quarter yellow plaid homespun or flannel
- 1 fat quarter pink plaid homespun or flannel
- 1 fat quarter blue plaid homespun or flannel
- 1/2 yard cotton batting
- All-purpose thread to match fabrics
- Light brown 6-strand embroidery floss
- Basic sewing tools and supplies, embroidery needle, rotary cutter, mat and ruler, and water-erasable marker or pencil

Instructions

Step 1. Cut two 10" x 10" squares and three 4" x 10" rectangles each multicolor plaid and yellow plaid homespun or flannel.

Step 2. Cut one 5" x 22" strip pink plaid homespun or flannel.

Step 3. Cut two 8" x 8" squares, three 2" x 8" rectangles and one 2" x 21" strip cotton batting.

Step 4. Center and sandwich the 8" x 8" batting square between one multicolor plaid and one yellow plaid 10" x 10" square; repeat with second set of squares.

Step 5. Mark and stitch each layered square referring to Steps 5 and 6 for Teddy Bear Quilt.

Step 6. Center and layer the 2" x 8" batting rectangles with the 4" x 10" fabric rectangles to make gusset pieces.

Step 7. Mark and stitch each layered gusset piece as in Step 5.

Step 8. Prepare patterns for small bear pieces using patterns given; cut as directed on each piece.

Step 9. Layer two ear pieces with wrong sides together; stitch around curved sides using a 1/2" seam allowance. Sew the ears to two top angled edges of the head piece with wrong sides together using a 1/2" seam allowance.

Step 10. Center and pin the head/ear shape on one stitched-and-layered square. Stitch in place, leaving a 1/2" seam allowance all around.

Step 11. Join the three gusset pieces on short ends with yellow sides together using a 1" seam allowance.

Step 12. Pin the gusset strip around three sides of the appliquéd square with yellow sides together as shown in Figure 3; stitch using a 1" seam allowance. Repeat with the remaining layered square. Stitch around top of bag 1" from outer edge.

Teddy Bear Tote
Placement Diagram
8" x 8" x 2"

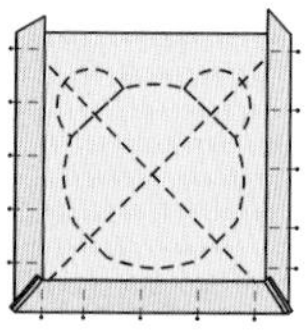

Figure 3
Pin the gusset strip around 3 sides of the appliquéd square with yellow sides together.

Step 13. Press under 1/4" along long edges and each end of the 5" x 22" strip pink plaid. Center the 2" x 21" strip batting on the wrong side of the strip; fold sides over batting, overlapping as needed. Stitch along overlapped seam and 1/4" from all edges as shown in Figure 4 to complete strap.

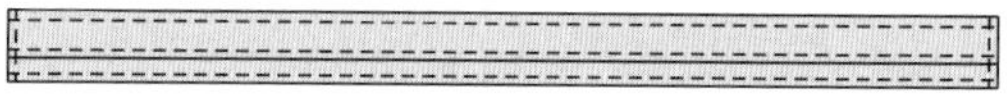

Figure 4
Stitch along overlapped seam and 1/4" from all edges.

Step 14. Pin and stitch strap ends to top inside edges of the stitched bag; stitch in place.

Step 15. Clip outside edge and each seam to within 1/8" of the stitched line every scant 1/4". Repeat on bear shape seams and outer edge.

Step 16. Wash and dry the bag to make edges fringe; remove all loose threads.

Step 17. Using 2 strands of light brown embroidery floss, blanket-stitch the eyes and nose in place on the bear/ear shape. Chain-stitch a mouth using drawing given to finish. ❖

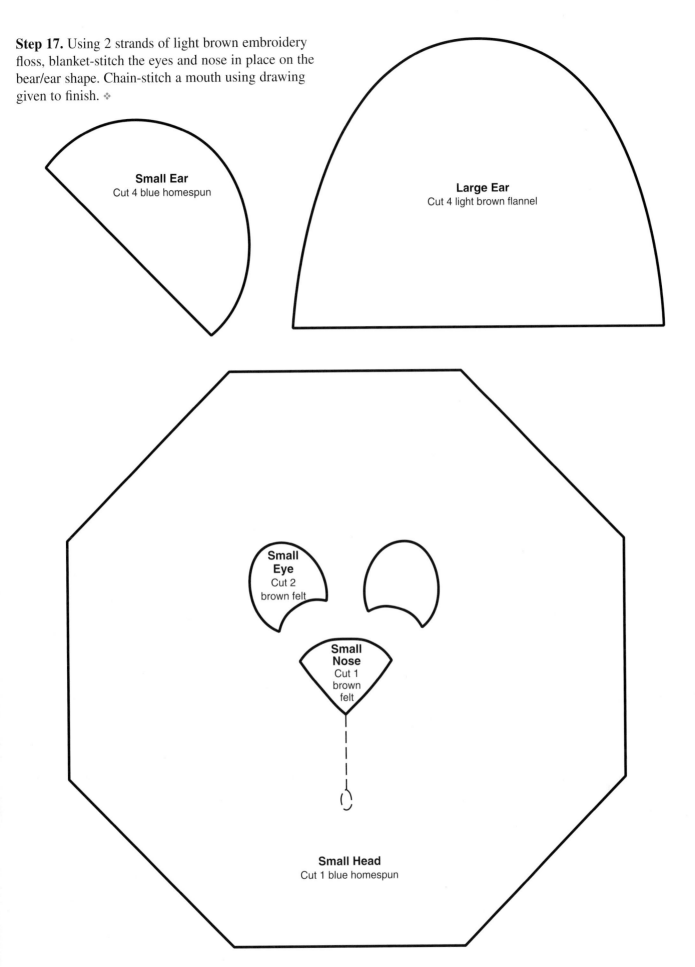

Small Ear
Cut 4 blue homespun

Large Ear
Cut 4 light brown flannel

Small Eye
Cut 2 brown felt

Small Nose
Cut 1 brown felt

Small Head
Cut 1 blue homespun

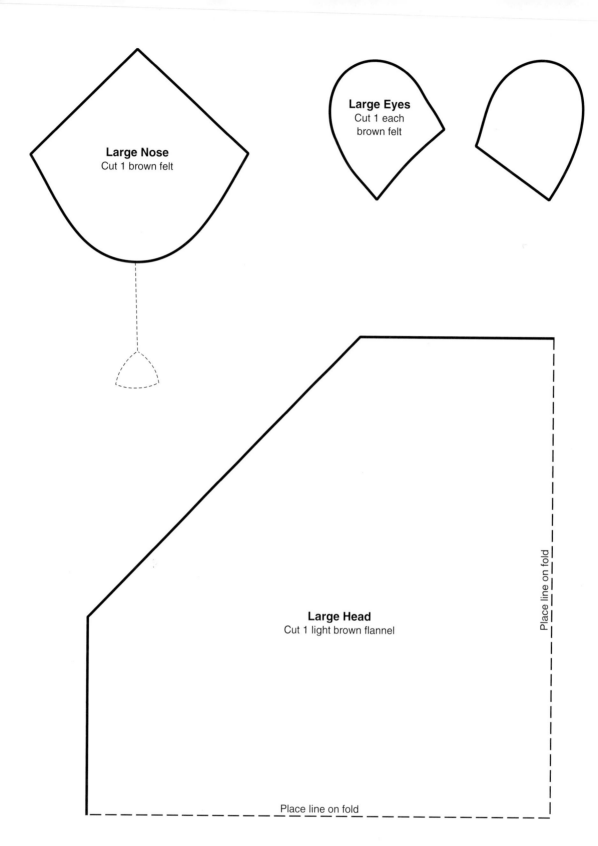

Large Nose
Cut 1 brown felt

Large Eyes
Cut 1 each
brown felt

Large Head
Cut 1 light brown flannel

Place line on fold

Place line on fold

Celebration

By Sue Harvey

A variation of the Kansas Dugout block is used in two different color arrangements to make a very happy quilt.

Project Notes

This quilt is made with two different block color placements, Celebration 1 block and Celebration 2 block. Each Celebration 1 block uses one main bright color for the corners and center, and four different bright colors for the diamond-shape pieces (diamond units). Each Celebration 2 block uses one main bright color for the side centers, and five different bright colors for the diamond-shape pieces (diamond units).

Each diamond shape is actually made as four corner triangles are joined. Be careful when choosing the colors for each block to use four of the same bright-color D pieces to create each diamond shape.

Project Specifications

Skill Level: Intermediate
Quilt Size: 54" x 72"
Block Size: 9" x 9"
Number of Blocks: 35

Materials

- 18 bright-colored print fat quarters
- 4 1/2 yards white-on-white print
- Batting 58" x 76"
- Backing 58" x 76"
- All-purpose thread to match fabrics
- Basic sewing tools and supplies, rotary cutter, mat and ruler

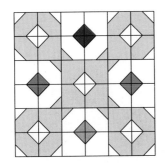

Celebration 1
9" x 9" Block

Celebration 2
9" x 9" Block

Instructions

Note: Fabrics will be referred to as bright or white throughout these instructions.

Step 1. Cut two strips each 2" x 48 1/2" and 2" x 63 1/2" from length of white; set aside for borders.

Step 2. Cut 51 strips white 1 1/4" by remaining fabric width and three strips 1 1/4" by full fabric width; sub-cut each strip into 1 1/4" square segments for B. You will need 1,460 B squares.

Step 3. Cut 30 strips white 2" by full fabric width; subcut each strip into 2" square segments for C. You will need 628 C squares.

Step 4. From each fat quarter, cut six strips 2" x 22"; subcut each strip into 2" square segments for A. You will need 56 A squares from each fat quarter.

Step 5. From each fat quarter, cut four strips 1 1/4" x 22"; cut each strip into 1 1/4" square segments for D. You will need 52 D squares from each fat quarter.

Step 6. Mark a diagonal line from corner to corner on the wrong side of each B and D square.

Step 7. To piece one Celebration 1 block, choose 20 same-bright A squares for the block main bright color. You will need eight main-bright D squares and four D squares each of four different bright colors to piece the block.

Step 8. Place B on opposite corners of A as shown in Figure 1; stitch on the marked line, trim seam allowance to 1/4" and press B open as shown in Figure 2. Repeat to make 12 A-B-B units.

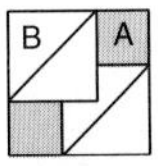

Figure 1
Place B on opposite corners of A.

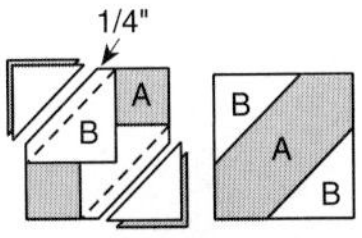

Figure 2
Stitch, trim and press open.

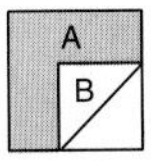

Figure 3
Place B on 1 corner of A.

Step 9. Repeat Step 8 except place B on only one corner of A as shown in Figure 3 to make an A-B unit; repeat to make eight A-B units.

Step 10. Join three A-B-B units with one A-B unit to make a bright corner unit as shown in Figure 4; repeat to make four bright corner units.

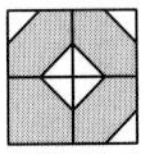

Figure 4
Make a bright corner unit as shown.

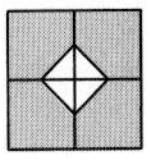

Figure 5
Make the bright center unit as shown.

Step 11. Join four A-B units to make the bright center unit as shown in Figure 5.

Step 12. Place a bright D on one corner of C as shown in Figure 6; stitch, trim and press open. Repeat for four same-bright C-D units.

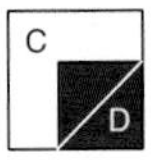

Figure 6
Place a bright D on 1 corner of C.

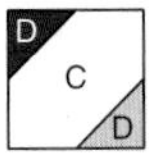

Figure 7
Make a C-D-D unit as shown.

Step 13. Place a main-bright D on the opposite corner of a C-D unit as shown in Figure 7; stitch, trim and press open. Repeat for two C-D-D units.

Step 14. Join the four pieced units to make one diamond unit as shown in Figure 8; repeat to make four diamond units using a different bright D in the center of each unit, again referring to Figure 8.

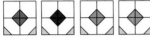

Figure 8
Make diamond units as shown.

Step 15. Join the bright corner units, bright center unit and diamond units in rows as shown in Figure 9; join the rows to complete one Celebration 1 block. Repeat to make 18 blocks, using a different bright for the main color of each block.

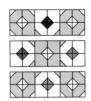

Figure 9
Join units in rows to complete 1 Celebration 1 block.

Step 16. To piece one Celebration 2 block, choose 16 same-bright A squares for the block main bright color. You will need eight main-bright D squares and four D squares each of five different bright colors to piece the block.

Step 17. Make eight A-B-B units referring to Step 8.

Step 18. Make eight A-B units referring to Step 9.

Step 19. Join two A-B-B units with two A-B units to make a bright side unit as shown in Figure 10; repeat for four bright side units.

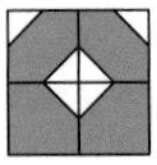

Figure 10
Make a bright side unit as shown.

Step 20. Make four same-bright C-D units referring to Step 12; repeat to make five different sets of four same-bright C-D units.

Step 21. Make one C-D-D unit each of four brights and four C-D-D units of the fifth bright referring to Step 13 and Figure 11.

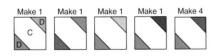

Figure 11
Make C-D-D units as shown.

Step 22. Join three same-bright C-D units with the same-bright C-D-D unit to make a corner diamond unit as shown in Figure 12; repeat for four corner diamond units.

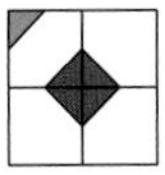

Figure 12
Make a corner diamond unit as shown.

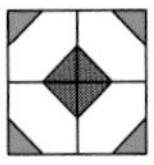

Figure 13
Make the center diamond unit as shown.

Step 23. Join the four same-bright C-D-D units to make the center diamond unit as shown in Figure 13.

Step 24. Join the bright side units and corner and center diamond units in rows as shown in Figure 14; join the rows to complete one Celebration 2 block. Repeat to make 17 blocks, using a different bright for the main color of each block.

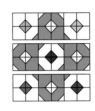

Figure 14
Join units in rows to complete 1 Celebration 2 block.

Step 25. Join three Celebration 1 blocks with two Celebration 2 blocks to make an A row as shown in Figure 15; repeat for four A rows.

Figure 15
Complete an A row as shown.

Step 26. Join two Celebration 1 blocks with three Celebration 2 blocks to make a B row as shown in Figure 16; repeat for three B rows.

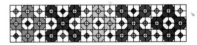

Figure 16
Complete a B row as shown.

Step 27. Join the rows to complete the pieced center, beginning and ending with an A row.

Step 28. Sew the longer border strips cut in Step 1 to opposite long sides of the pieced center and the shorter strips to the top and bottom; press seams toward strips.

Step 29. To make the pieced borders, make two A-B-B units and two A-B units using the same-bright A squares and referring to Steps 8 and 9. Join the units to make a bright side unit referring to Step 19. Repeat to make 76 bright side units. Make three A-B units and one A-B-B unit using the same-bright A squares. Join the units to make a corner diamond unit; repeat for four units. Set aside remaining A and D squares for another project.

Step 30. Join 22 bright side units to make a strip referring to the Placement Diagram for positioning; repeat for two strips.

Step 31. Sew a strip to opposite sides of the pieced center; press seams toward strips.

Step 32. Join 16 bright side units to make a strip; repeat for two strips. Sew a corner diamond unit to each end of each strip; sew a strip to the top and bottom to complete the pieced top.

Step 33. Prepare for quilting and quilt as desired referring to the General Instructions. *Note: The sample shown was professionally machine-quilted in an allover pattern.*

Step 34. Prepare 7 1/2 yards self-made white-on-white print binding and apply referring to the General Instructions. ❖

Celebration
Placement Diagram
54" x 72"

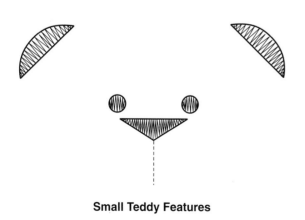

Teddy-Go-Round

Continued from page 10

Step 29. Quilt as desired. *Note: The sample shown was professionally machine-quilted in an allover pattern.*

Step 30. Prepare 5 1/2 yards self-made bear print binding and apply referring to the General Instructions. ❖

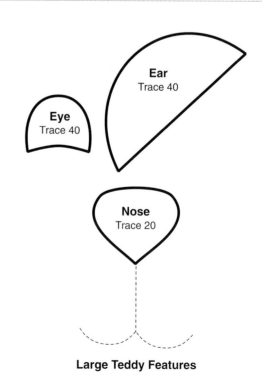

Eye
Trace 40

Ear
Trace 40

Nose
Trace 20

Small Teddy Features

Large Teddy Features

Baby Blocks With Love

By Judith Sandstrom

The heart design in this quilt does not reveal itself until the blocks are sewn together in rows.

Project Specifications

Skill Level: Beginner

Quilt Size: 40" x 56"

Block Size: 8" x 8"

Number of Blocks: 24

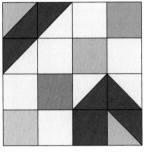

Block A
8" x 8" Block

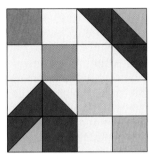

Block B
8" x 8" Block

Materials

- 1 fat quarter each peach, green, orange and blue tone-on-tones
- 1 fat quarter blue print
- 1/2 yard blue print for binding
- 1 yard cream-on-cream print
- 1 1/2 yards dark blue solid
- Batting 44" x 60"
- Backing 44" x 60"
- All-purpose thread to match fabrics
- Cream hand-quilting thread
- Basic sewing tools and supplies, rotary cutter, mat and ruler, and marking pencil

Instructions

Step 1. Cut two strips each 2 1/2" x 40 1/2" and 2 1/2" x 48 1/2" dark blue solid along the length of the fabric; set aside for borders.

Step 2. Cut six 2 1/2" x 22" strips from each tone-on-tone.

Step 3. Cut eight 2 1/2" by fabric width strips cream-on-cream print. Cut each strip in half to make sixteen 2 1/2" x 21" strips. Subcut three of these strips into 2 1/2" squares for A; you will need 24 A squares.

Step 4. Cut three strips dark blue solid 2 1/2" x 21"; subcut into 24 squares 2 1/2" x 2 1/2" for A.

Step 5. Sew one tone-on-tone strip to one cream-on-cream print strip with right sides together along length; repeat for three of each color tone-on-tone. Press seams toward darker fabric.

Step 6. Subcut each strip set into 2 1/2" segments to make B units as shown in Figure 1; you will need 24 B units of each tone-on-tone fabric.

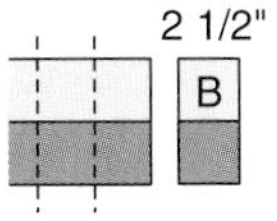

Figure 1
Subcut each strip set
into 2 1/2" segments
to make B units.

Figure 2
Subcut each strip set
into 2 1/2" segments
to make C units.

Step 7. Stitch one strip of each tone-on-tone with right sides together along length to make a strip set; press seams in one direction. Repeat for three strip sets. Subcut each strip set into 2 1/2" segments to make C units as shown in Figure 2; you will need 20 C units.

Step 8. Cut seven strips cream-on-cream print, four strips blue print and 11 strips dark blue solid 2 7/8" x 21". Subcut each strip into 2 7/8" square segments; you will need 48 squares cream-on-cream print, 24 squares blue print and 72 squares dark blue solid. Cut each square in half on one diagonal to make D triangles.

Step 9. Stitch each blue print D to a dark blue solid D to make a D unit as shown in Figure 3; repeat for all blue print D triangles. Repeat with remaining dark blue solid D triangles and cream-on-cream print D triangles, again referring to Figure 3.

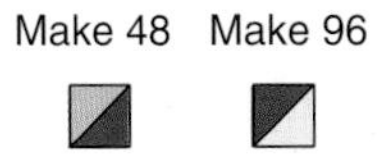

Make 48   Make 96

Figure 3
Join D pieces as shown.

Step 10. Arrange the A squares and B and D units in rows referring to Figure 4 for Blocks A and B. Join units in rows; join rows to complete one block. Repeat for 12 each A and B blocks; press seams open.

Step 11. Arrange blocks in six rows of four blocks each, alternating the A and B blocks as shown in Figure 5. Join blocks in rows; press seams open. Join rows to complete the quilt center; press seams open.

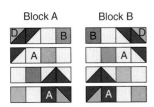

Block A   Block B

Figure 4
Arrange the A squares
and B and D units in
rows for Blocks A and B.

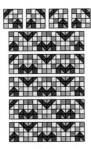

Figure 5
Arrange blocks in 6
rows of 4 blocks
each, alternating the
A and B blocks.

Step 12. Join four C units to make a border strip; repeat for two strips. Join six C units to make a side border strip; repeat for two strips.

Step 13. Sew a 2 1/2" x 48 1/2" strip dark blue solid to one six-unit side border strip; press seams away from the pieced strip. Repeat for two strips. Sew a strip to opposite sides of the pieced center with the dark blue solid strip on the inside edge referring to Figure 6; press seams toward dark blue solid strip. Repeat on the opposite long side of the quilt center.

2 1/2" x 48 1/2"

Figure 6
Sew a strip to opposite
sides of the pieced center
with the dark blue solid
strip on the inside edge.

Step 14. Cut four squares 2 1/2" x 2 1/2" each blue print and dark blue solid. Sew a dark blue solid square and a blue print square to each end of the four-unit strips as shown in Figure 7. Sew a 2 1/2" x 40 1/2" strip dark blue solid to each pieced strip as in Step 13; press seams toward dark blue solid strips. Sew a strip to the top and bottom of the pieced center; press seams toward dark blue solid strips.

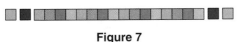

Figure 7
Sew a dark blue solid square and a blue
print square to each end of the 4-unit strips.

Step 15. Prepare quilt for quilting and quilt as desired referring to the General Instructions. *Note: The sample*

2" x 40"

Baby Blocks With Love
Placement Diagram
40" x 56"

shown was hand-quilted around the heart shapes and in a diagonal line through the center of each block and in the ditch of border seams using cream hand-quilting thread.

Step 16. Prepare 5 3/4 yards self-made blue print binding and apply referring to the General Instructions. ❖

Christmas Keepsakes

Cardinals, poinsettias, stockings and wreaths fill your home with joy as you stitch these keepsake quilts and projects from fat quarters to give as gifts to those you love.

Checkerboard Four-Patch

By Sandra L. Hatch

Red and green metallic prints add a richness to this Christmas quilt.

Project Specifications

Skill Level: Beginner

Quilt Size: 88" x 104"

Block Sizes: 16" x 16"

Number of Blocks: 20

Checkerboard Four-Patch
16" x 16" Block

Materials

◆ 10 fat quarters cream and off-white prints and tone-on-tones

◆ 12 fat quarters red-with-metallic prints

◆ 13 fat quarters green-with-metallic prints

◆ 3/4 yard cream print for borders

◆ 3/4 yard red print for borders

◆ 2 3/4 yards red-and-green metallic directional print or 1 3/8 yards non-directional print for outside border strips

◆ Batting 92" x 108"

◆ Backing 92" x 108"

◆ 11 yards self-made or purchased binding

◆ All-purpose thread to match fabrics

◆ Gold machine-quilting thread

◆ Basic sewing tools and supplies, rotary cutter, mat and ruler

Instructions

Note: The instructions will refer to fabrics by color not by listed name in the materials list.

Step 1. Cut two 4 1/2" x 96 1/2" strips red-and-green metallic border print along length of fabric. *Note: The print used on the quilt is a one-way design, requiring the strips be cut along the length of the fabric. If your fabric is not a directional print, strips may be cut across the width of the fabric and pieced for the sides.* Cut and piece two 4 1/2" x 88 1/2" strips red-and-green metallic border print. Set aside border strips. Remainder of border fabric may be used in piecing blocks.

Step 2. Cut ten 4 1/2" x 22" strips each red and green fat quarters. *Note: Cut one strip each from 10 different red and green fat quarters.*

Step 3. Sew a green strip to a red strip with right sides together along length; press seams toward green print strips. Subcut strip sets into 4 1/2" segments as shown in Figure 1; you will need 40 segments.

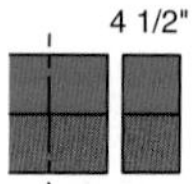

Figure 1
Subcut strip sets into 4 1/2" segments.

Figure 2
Join 2 segments to make a Four-Patch unit.

Step 4. Join two segments as shown in Figure 2 to make a Four-Patch unit; repeat for 20 Four-Patch units. Press seams in one direction.

Step 5. Cut 40 squares off-white or cream fat quarters 6 5/8" x 6 5/8". Cut each square in half on one diagonal to make A triangles. You will need 80 A triangles.

Step 6. Sew four same-fabric A triangles to each Four-Patch unit as shown in Figure 3; press seams toward A.

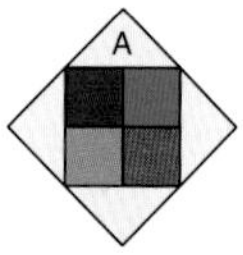

Figure 3
Sew 4 same-fabric A triangles to each Four-Patch unit.

Step 7. Cut 21 strips 2 1/2" x 22" each green and red fat quarters. Sew a green strip to a red strip with right sides together along length; press seams toward green print strips. Repeat for 21 strip sets.

Step 8. Subcut strip sets into 2 1/2" segments as shown in Figure 4; you will need 168 segments.

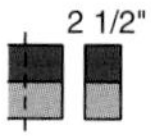

Figure 4
Subcut strip sets into 2 1/2" segments.

Figure 5
Join 2 segments to make a Four-Patch unit.

Step 9. Join two segments to make a Four-Patch unit as shown in Figure 5; press seams in one direction. You will need 84 Four-Patch units; set aside 80 for blocks and four for borders.

Step 10. Cut 20 strips 2 1/2" x 22" off-white or cream fat quarters; subcut strips into 2 1/2" squares for B. You will need 160 B squares.

Step 11. Cut 23 strips red fat quarters 2 7/8" x 22"; subcut strips into 2 7/8" square segments. Cut each square in half on one diagonal to make C triangles. You will need 320 C triangles.

Step 12. Sew two C triangles to adjacent sides of B as shown in Figure 6; repeat for 160 B-C units.

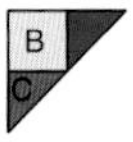

Figure 6
Sew 2 C triangles to
adjacent sides of B.

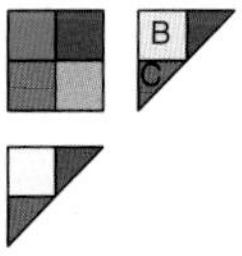

Figure 7
Sew a B-C unit to 2
adjacent sides of a
Four-Patch unit.

Step 13. Sew a B-C unit to two adjacent sides of a Four-Patch unit as shown in Figure 7; repeat for 80 units.

Step 14. Sew a B-C/Four-Patch unit to each side of an A unit to complete one block as shown in Figure 8; repeat for 20 blocks.

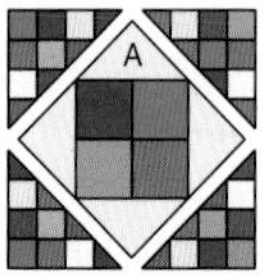

Figure 8
Sew a B-C/Four-Patch
unit to each side of an A
unit to complete 1 block.

Step 15. Join four blocks to make a row; repeat for five rows. Press seams in one direction. Join the rows to complete the pieced center; press seams in one direction.

Step 16. Cut and piece two strips each cream and red print border fabrics 2 1/2" x 64 1/2" and 2 1/2" x 80 1/2". Sew a 64 1/2" cream print strip to a 64 1/2" red print strip with right sides together along length; press seam toward red print strip. Repeat for two strips. Sew these strips to the top and bottom of the pieced center; press seams toward strips.

Step 17. Sew an 80 1/2" cream print strip to an 80 1/2" red print strip with right sides together along length; press seam toward red print strip. Repeat for two strips. Sew a Four-Patch unit set aside in Step 9 to each end of each strip; sew these strips to opposite long sides of the pieced center. Press seams toward strips.

Step 18. Cut 20 strips 4 1/2" x 22" green fat quarters; subcut into 4 1/2" square segments for D. You will need 80 D squares. Join 22 D squares to make a side strip; repeat for two side strips. Press seams in one direction. Sew a strip to opposite long sides of the pieced center; press seams toward strips.

Step 19. Cut four squares 4 1/2" x 4 1/2" from red fat quarters. Join 18 green squares to make a strip: add a red square to each end to make the top strip. Repeat for bottom strip. Press seams in one direction; sew a strip to the top and bottom of the pieced center; press seams toward strips.

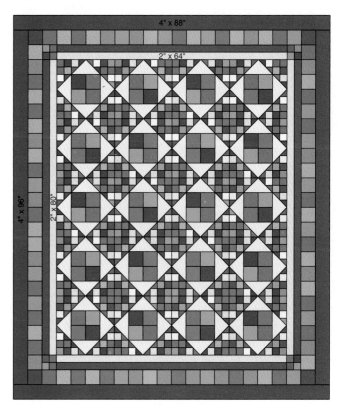

Checkerboard Four-Patch
Placement Diagram
88" x 104"

Step 20. Sew the 96 1/2" strips cut in Step 1 to opposite long sides and the 88 1/2" strips to the top and bottom of the pieced center; press seams toward strips.

Step 21. Prepare for quilting and quilt as desired referring to the General Instructions. *Note: The quilt shown was professionally machine-quilted in a meandering pattern using gold machine-quilting thread.*

Step 22. Apply self-made or purchased binding referring to the General Instructions to finish. ❖

Nativity Wall Quilt

By Barbara Clayton

Make a fabric nativity scene using fat quarters and scraps.

Project Specifications

Skill Level: Intermediate

Quilt Size: 17" x 19"

Materials

- 2" x 3" scrap white solid for baby clothes
- 3" x 3" scrap peach solid for faces and hands
- 3" x 3" scrap navy solid for Joseph's headband and inside sleeve
- 3" x 4" scrap medium blue print for Mary's hood
- 3" x 10" scrap dark brown print for staff and shoes
- 4" x 4" scrap tan print for manger highlights
- 4" x 4" scrap white-on-white print for lambs
- 4" x 4" scrap brown solid for hair
- 4" x 6" scrap dark red print for Joseph's hood and cape
- 5" x 5" scrap red print for Mary's gown
- 5" x 5" scrap yellow mottled for star and hay
- 5" x 6" scrap dark blue print for Joseph's robe
- 8" x 8" scrap gray mottled for stable rock walls
- 8" x 9" scrap black solid for stable and lamb faces and legs
- 8" x 16" scrap medium brown print for eaves and stable door openings and manger
- 8" x 16" scrap golden brown print for roof and stable posts
- 1 fat quarter navy-with-stars print for sky
- 1 fat quarter green print for ground
- 1 fat quarter gold print for binding, halo and star shadows
- Batting 17 1/2" x 23"
- Backing 17 1/2" x 23"
- All-purpose thread to match fabrics
- Black machine-quilting thread
- Clear nylon monofilament
- 1 yard fusible transfer web
- 17" x 19" piece fabric stabilizer
- Gold metallic thread
- 1/2 yard narrow gold metallic cord
- Basic sewing tools and supplies

Instructions

Step 1. Trace each shape onto the paper side of the fusible transfer web using full-size pattern given, adding 1/8" wherever pattern is covered by another piece and leaving a margin between pieces. *Note: The pattern is given full-size and reversed for fusible machine-appliqué.*

Step 2. Cut out shapes, leaving a margin around each one. Fuse shapes to the wrong side of the scraps and fat quarters referring to the listed materials for color of each shape.

Step 3. Cut out all fused shapes along traced lines; remove paper backing.

Step 4. Cut a 13 1/2" x 17 1/2" rectangle navy-with-stars print and a 6 1/2" x 17 1/2" rectangle green print. Sew the two rectangles with right sides together along the 17 1/2" edges; press. Pin the 17" x 19" piece of fabric stabilizer to the wrong side of the background piece.

Step 5. Cut a 5 1/2" x 9" rectangle black solid for stable. Bond a few pieces of fusible transfer web around outside edges; remove paper backing. Center the stable piece on the background with bottom edge 1 7/8" below the seam between the two background pieces as shown in Figure 1; fuse in place.

Step 6. Arrange the stable door openings, roof parts and rock walls around the black solid piece referring to Figure 2 and the pattern for order of appliqué.

Figure 1
Center the stable piece on the background with bottom edge 1 7/8" below the seam between the 2 background pieces.

Figure 2
Arrange the stable door openings, walls and roof parts around the black solid piece in numerical order.

Step 7. Using clear nylon monofilament in the top of the machine and all-purpose thread in the bobbin, stitch along raw edge of each shape using a narrow, close zigzag stitch.

Step 8. Arrange lamb pieces in numerical order on each side on the rock walls referring to the full-size drawing for placement; fuse and then stitch in place as in Step 7.

Step 9. Arrange the Mary, Joseph and Baby motif on the fused section in numerical order with the manger 1 3/4" from bottom edge; fuse shapes in place in numerical order. Stitch each piece in place as in Step 7.

Step 10. Cut pieces of narrow gold metallic cord to fit lines on the halo, referring to the lines on the pattern. Using gold metallic thread in the top of the machine and all-purpose thread in the bobbin, zigzag-stitch over cord pieces to hold in place. Repeat around outside edge of halo.

Step 11. Fuse star shape 4" from left edge and 1" from top edge as shown in Figure 3. Machine-stitch in place as in Step 7; remove fabric stabilizer.

Step 12. Draw radiating lines from the four points of the star to the edges of the quilt top and down to the ground or stable as shown in Figure 4. Repeat with four lines radiating from the four indentations of the star to the edges. Draw six radiating lines from the star between the previous eight lines referring to the Placement Diagram. Round buttom corners through all layers.

Nativity Wall Quilt
Placement Diagram
17" x 19"

Figure 3
Fuse star shape 4" from left
edge and 1" from top edge.

Figure 4
Draw radiating lines from the
star to edges as shown.

Step 13. Place the backing piece on a flat surface right side down; place the batting on top. Place the appliquéd top on the layers matching bottom edges and leaving all excess above the top edge as shown in Figure 5; pin or baste layers together.

Step 14. Cut a piece of navy-with-stars print 4 1/2" x 17 1/2". Pin the navy-with-stars strip right sides together with the top edge of the appliquéd top; stitch. Trim the

Figure 5
Place the appliquéd top on
the layers matching bottom
edges and leaving all
excess above the top edge.

batting even with seam on the inside; trim the backing 3/8" shorter than the appliquéd top along the top edge. Turn under top edge of strip 1/2"; press. Fold the top folded edge of the strip over the backing piece to cover trimmed edge and stitch in place as shown in Figure 6.

Figure 6
Fold the top folded edge of the strip
over the backing piece to cover
trimmed edge and stitch in place.

Step 15. Extend radiating lines from star into the top strip. Machine-quilt on the marked lines using gold metallic thread in the top of the machine and all-purpose thread in the bobbin. Machine-quilt on all detail lines, including eyes and hair, using black machine-quilting thread in the top of the machine and all-purpose thread in the bobbin.

Step 16. Prepare 2 1/4 yards gold mottled binding and apply to the side and bottom edges referring to the General Instructions.

Step 17. Turn the top edge of the quilted top to the backside 2" above seam; hand-stitch in place to make a hanging tube to finish. ❖

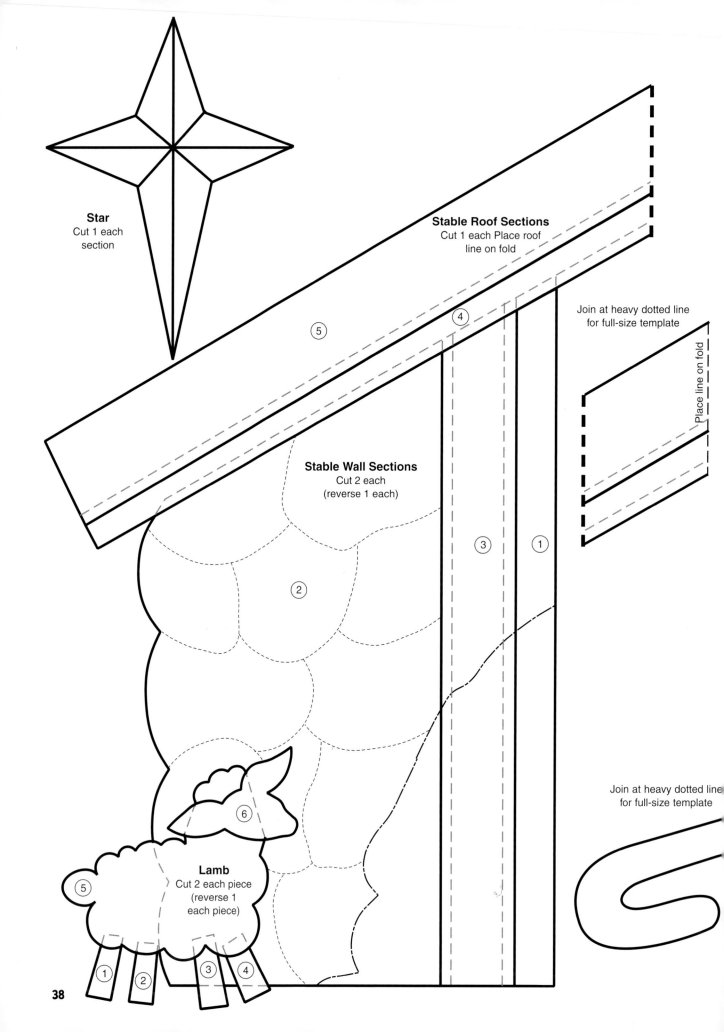

Star
Cut 1 each section

Stable Roof Sections
Cut 1 each Place roof line on fold

Join at heavy dotted line for full-size template

Place line on fold

⑤

④

Stable Wall Sections
Cut 2 each (reverse 1 each)

③ ①

②

Join at heavy dotted line for full-size template

⑥

Lamb
Cut 2 each piece (reverse 1 each piece)

⑤

① ② ③ ④

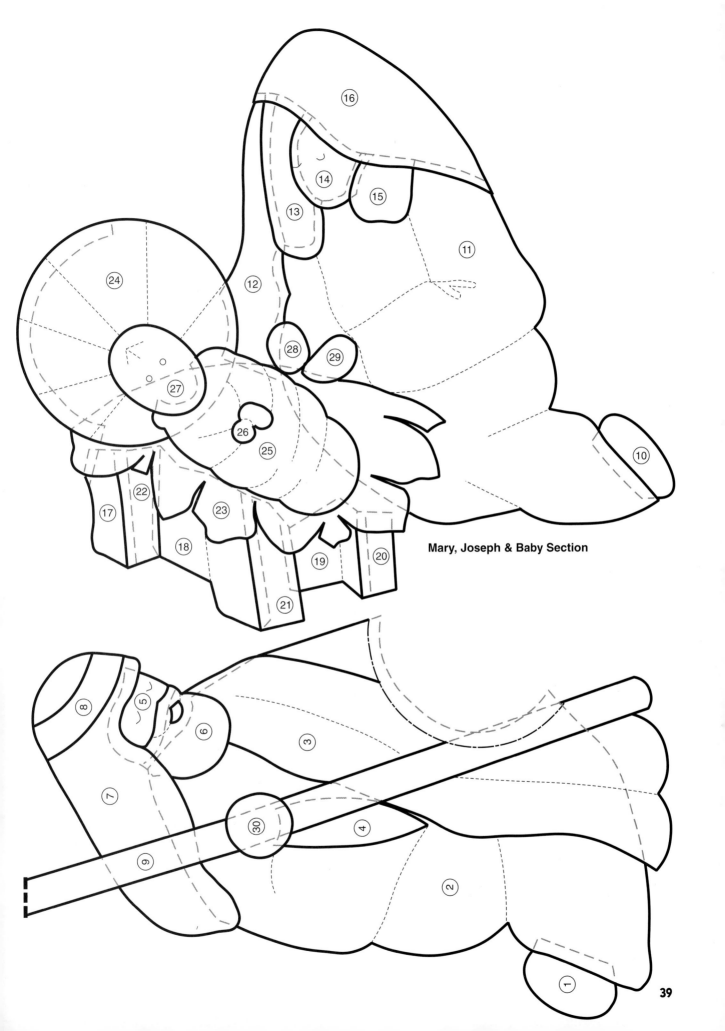

Mary, Joseph & Baby Section

Christmas Cardinal

By Willow Ann Sirch

The cardinal among patchwork evergreen branches is an expression of the spirit of thankfulness.

Cardinal
8" x 8" Block

Evergreen
8" x 8" Block

Project Notes

This project features a kind of "paint-by-number" approach for the cardinal motifs adapted from Carol Armstrong's book *Wild Birds: Designs for Appliqué and Quilting*. A foundation-pieced quilt block known as the Palm Leaf creates the evergreen branches. The fabrics used include tiny-print calicos, speckled prints, solids and hand-dyed cottons. A touch of gold in the border fabrics says, "Christmas."

The project is for intermediate to advanced quilters because of its combination of detailed appliqué with foundation piecing. If you have never tried foundation piecing, this project, with only three foundation-pieced blocks, might be a good way to test the waters. A small, inexpensive light box may be purchased at many craft stores for under $10.

Accuracy is especially important when creating paper-piecing patterns. Photocopy machines sometimes distort images. For that reason, the foundation pattern pieces for the evergreen blocks were individually measured and marked on graph paper before being cut out.

A second method for reproducing the foundation pattern pieces is to trace the pattern onto a piece of tracing paper. Layer the traced design with seven or eight additional sheets of tracing paper and sew over the marked design with an unthreaded sewing machine.

If you must photocopy the patterns, be sure to copy all of them at the same time using the same machine. You will need two copies for each evergreen block—a total of six copies for the three blocks. Number the shapes on each foundation paper as on the templates. The numbers indicate sewing order.

Project Specifications

Skill Level: Intermediate

Quilt Size: 28" x 36"

Block Size: 8" x 8"

Number of Blocks: 6

Materials

◆ 4" x 4" scrap light red fabric

◆ 3" x 3" scrap black fabric

◆ 3" x 4" scrap dark orange fabric

◆ 1 fat quarter medium red fabric

◆ 1 fat quarter brown fabric

◆ 1 fat quarter light green fabric

◆ 6–8 different dark red-to-maroon fat quarters or large scraps

◆ 1 dark and 2 medium green fat quarters

◆ 1/3 yard gold print

◆ 1/2 yard maroon-with-gold specks

◆ 3/4 yard muslin

◆ Backing 32" x 40"

◆ Batting 32" x 40"

◆ 4 yards self-made red/gold binding

◆ All-purpose thread to match fabrics

◆ Off-white hand-quilting thread

◆ 1 skein each medium and dark green 6-strand embroidery floss

◆ Embroidery needle and small hoop

◆ Light box

◆ Water-erasable marker

◆ Basic sewing supplies and tools

Instructions

Making Evergreen Blocks

Step 1. Copy paper-piecing patterns for the Evergreen blocks using the patterns given; you need three of each paper-piecing pattern for blocks and one of each extra to cut into individual pieces.

Step 2. Cut apart the extra patterns completely and lay out pieces in the correct sewing order.

Step 3. Measure the widest point of the longest triangle shape and add an inch or more to the measurement; cut strips from each green fat quarter and muslin in that size. Cut out the triangle shapes for each block from the strips in their sewing order, allowing at least 1/2" extra all around each shape for seams.

Step 4. Pin a numbered, cut-out paper pattern piece to each shape for identification.

Step 5. Place fabric shape 1 right side up on the unmarked side of one A side of a foundation paper pattern as shown in Figure 1. Holding the foundation paper with pinned piece up to the light box or a table lamp, check to see that shape 1 covers the area marked 1 on the foundation paper. Pin shape 2 on shape 1 on the 2 side of 1 with right sides together as shown in Figure 2.

Figure 1
Place shape 1 right side up on the unmarked A side of the pattern.

Figure 2
Pin shape 2 right sides together with shape 1.

Step 6. With marked side of foundation paper up, sew on the line between shapes 1 and 2 as shown in Figure 3. Flip shape 2 flat to be sure it covers all of area 2 on the paper as shown in Figure 4; press light seams toward dark. Trim excess seam allowance between pieces to 1/4".

Figure 3
Flip pattern and stitch on the 1-2 line.

Figure 4
Press shape 2 flat, covering all of area 2.

Step 7. Continue adding pieces in this manner in numerical order until the foundation piece is covered. Repeat for B section of the same block.

Step 8. Join the two half sections as shown in Figure 5 to complete one block; repeat for one dark green and two medium green blocks. Press each block. Trim any excess from outside edges 1/4" from drawn paper lines; set aside.

Figure 5
Join 2 half sections to complete 1 block.

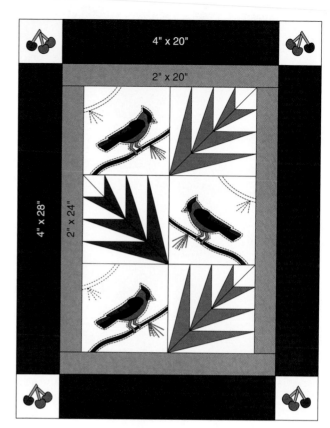

Christmas Cardinal
Placement Diagram
28" x 36"

Making Cardinal Blocks

Step 1. Copy three cardinal designs using drawing given, reversing one design motif; tape one design to the light box.

Step 2. Cut three 8 1/2" x 8 1/2" squares muslin. Tape a muslin square over the design on the light box. ***Note:*** *If you don't have a light box, use a window during daylight hours.*

Step 3. Using a water-erasable marker, lightly trace the cardinal pattern onto two muslin squares; repeat with reversed design on one square. Transfer numbers from the pattern pieces to the muslin squares and set aside.

Step 4. With the cardinal paper pattern still taped to the light box, use the water-erasable marker to mark each shape on the right side of the chosen fabrics. Use medium red for the cardinal's body, light red for the head crest, black for the face, dark orange for the beak and legs, and brown for the branch. Use the dark red-to-maroon fabrics for the cardinal's wing and tail feathers. Cut out the shapes, allowing a 1/4" seam allowance all around.

Step 5. Pin and needle-turn appliqué the branch and cardinal shapes in place on each muslin block in the correct sewing order. ***Note:*** *The raw edges of some shapes are cov-*

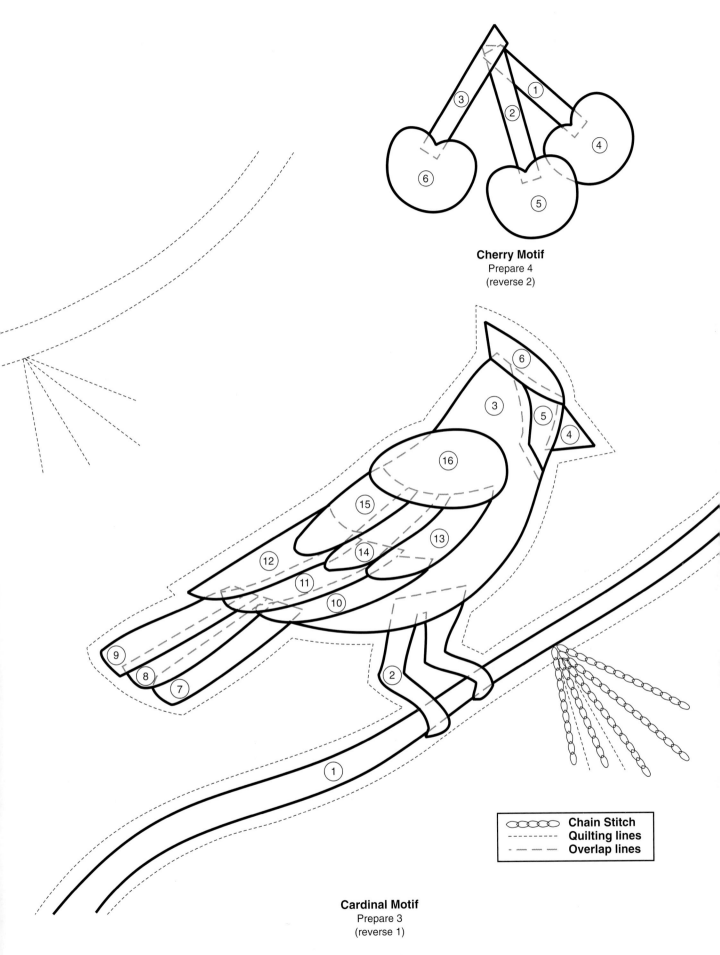

Cherry Motif
Prepare 4
(reverse 2)

Chain Stitch
Quilting lines
Overlap lines

Cardinal Motif
Prepare 3
(reverse 1)

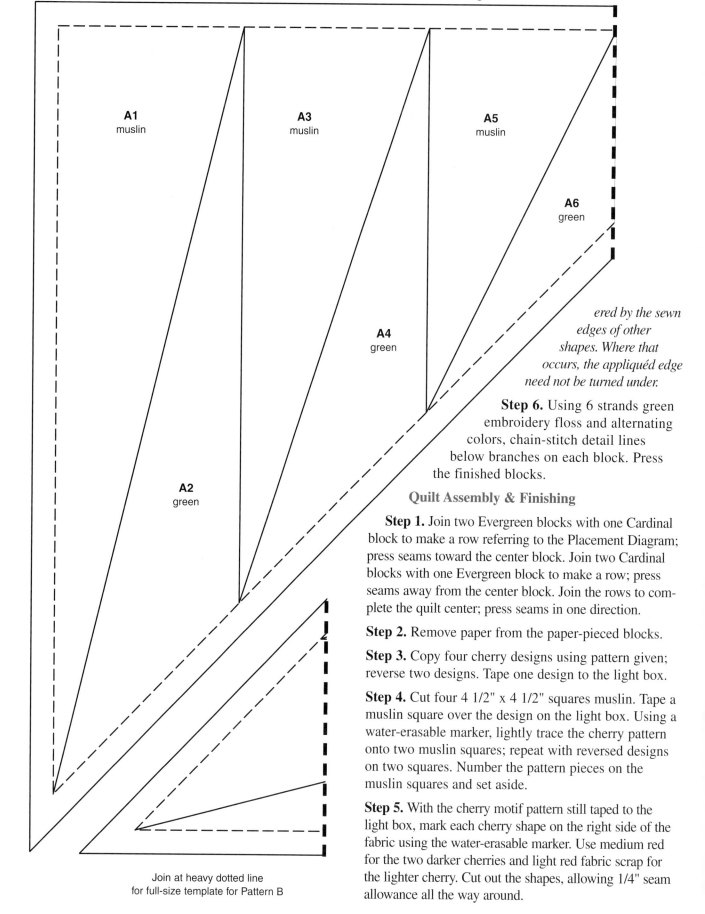

Evergreen Foundation-Piecing Pattern A

A1
muslin

A3
muslin

A5
muslin

A6
green

A4
green

A2
green

Join at heavy dotted line
for full-size template for Pattern B

*ered by the sewn
edges of other
shapes. Where that
occurs, the appliquéd edge
need not be turned under.*

Step 6. Using 6 strands green
embroidery floss and alternating
colors, chain-stitch detail lines
below branches on each block. Press
the finished blocks.

Quilt Assembly & Finishing

Step 1. Join two Evergreen blocks with one Cardinal
block to make a row referring to the Placement Diagram;
press seams toward the center block. Join two Cardinal
blocks with one Evergreen block to make a row; press
seams away from the center block. Join the rows to complete the quilt center; press seams in one direction.

Step 2. Remove paper from the paper-pieced blocks.

Step 3. Copy four cherry designs using pattern given;
reverse two designs. Tape one design to the light box.

Step 4. Cut four 4 1/2" x 4 1/2" squares muslin. Tape a
muslin square over the design on the light box. Using a
water-erasable marker, lightly trace the cherry pattern
onto two muslin squares; repeat with reversed designs
on two squares. Number the pattern pieces on the
muslin squares and set aside.

Step 5. With the cherry motif pattern still taped to the
light box, mark each cherry shape on the right side of the
fabric using the water-erasable marker. Use medium red
for the two darker cherries and light red fabric scrap for
the lighter cherry. Cut out the shapes, allowing 1/4" seam
allowance all the way around.

Step 6. Cut four 3/8" x 6" strips light green. Fold both long edges under a scant 1/8" and secure with a single line of basting; press. Cut the basted strips to size for stems referring to pattern; appliqué in place in the correct sewing order, covering the raw stem ends with another stem or cherries, except for the top stem which may be turned under on the exposed end. Pin and needle-turn appliqué the cherries in place in the correct sewing order.

Step 7. Cut two strips each gold print 2 1/2" x 20 1/2" and 2 1/2" x 24 1/2". Sew the longer strips to opposite sides and shorter strips to the top and bottom of the pieced center; press seams toward strips.

Step 8. Cut two strips each 4 1/2" x 20 1/2" and 4 1/2" x 28 1/2" maroon-with-gold specks. Sew the longer strips to opposite sides of the pieced center; press seams toward strips. Sew a Cherry block to both ends of each of the remaining gold print strips; press seams toward darker fabric. Sew to the top and bottom of the pieced center; press seams toward strips.

Step 9. Prepare for quilting and quilt as desired referring to the General Instructions. *Note: The quilt shown was hand-quilted 1/4" around appliqué motifs and pieced seams, and in a branch and needle shape in the top corner of each Cardinal block using off-white hand-quilting thread.*

Step 10. Apply self-made or purchased binding referring to the General Instructions to finish. ❖

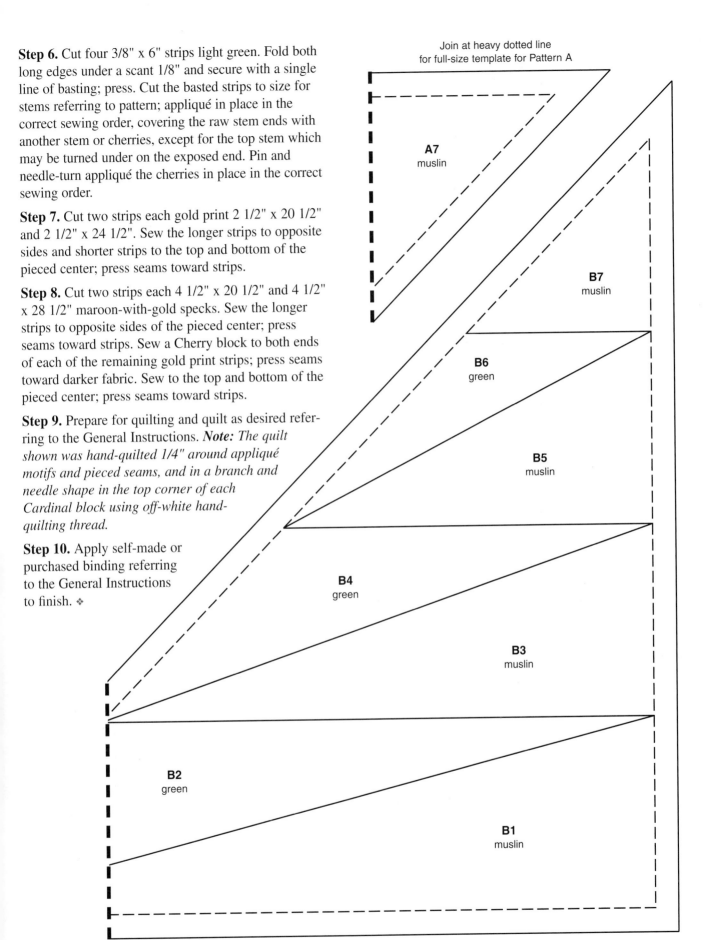

Join at heavy dotted line
for full-size template for Pattern A

A7
muslin

B7
muslin

B6
green

B5
muslin

B4
green

B3
muslin

B2
green

B1
muslin

Evergreen Foundation-Piecing Pattern B

Sign of the Season

By Julie Weaver

Spread the message of Joy with a seasonal wall banner.

Project Specifications

Skill Level: Intermediate

Quilt Size: 23" x 41"

Block Sizes: 5" x 5" and 5" x 7"

Number of Blocks: 14 and 3

Materials

- 1 fat quarter green tone-on-tone
- 1 fat quarter green mottled
- 2 fat quarters red tone-on-tones
- 1 yard cream-on-cream print
- Batting 27" x 45"
- Backing 27" x 45"
- 4 yards self-made or purchased binding
- All-purpose thread to match fabrics
- Cream machine-quilting thread
- Basic sewing tools and supplies, rotary cutter, mat and ruler

Instructions

Making Star Blocks

Step 1. Cut one strip 1 1/2" x 22" each red tone-on-tone. *Note: Choose which tone-on-tone fabric will be used for eight blocks (red 8) and which will be used for six blocks (red 6).* Subcut one red 8 strip into eight 1 1/2" segments for A8 and the red 6 strip into six 1 1/2" segments for A6.

Step 2. Cut three strips red 8 tone-on-tone 1 1/2" x 22" and two strips cream-on-cream print 1 1/2" by fabric width. Cut each cream-on-cream print strip in half to make four shorter strips; set aside one strip for another project. Sew each of the red strips to a cream-on-cream print strip with right sides together along length; press and subcut into 1 1/2" segments for B as shown in Figure 1. You will need 32 B8 segments.

Step 3. Cut two strips red 6 tone-on-tone 1 1/2" x 22" and one strip cream-on-cream print 1 1/2" by fabric width. Cut the cream-on-cream print strip in half to make two shorter strips. Sew each of the red strips to a cream-on-cream print strip with right sides together along length; press and subcut into 1 1/2" segments, again referring to Figure 1. You will need 24 B6 segments.

Step 4. Cut four 1 1/2" x 22" strips red 8 and three strips red 6; subcut strips into 2 1/2" segments for C. You will need 32 C8 and 24 C6 rectangles.

Step 5. Cut eight strips cream-on-cream print 1 1/2" by fabric width; subcut four strips into 1 1/2" segments for D and four strips into 2 1/2" segments for E. You will need 112 D and 56 E pieces. Draw a diagonal line from corner to corner on the wrong side of each D square.

Figure 1
Subcut strips into 1 1/2" segments for B8 and B6.

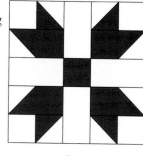

Star
5" x 5" Block

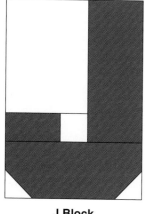

J Block
5" x 7" Block

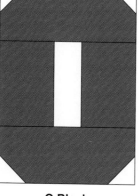

O Block
5" x 7" Block

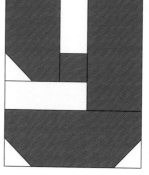

Y Block
5" x 7" Block

COLOR KEY
- ☐ Cream-on-cream print
- Red 6
- Red 8
- Green tone-on-tone
- Green mottled

Step 6. To make one red 8 Star block, place a D square right sides together on the left side of C8; stitch on the line as shown in Figure 2. Trim seam to 1/4" and press to the right side as shown in Figure 3; repeat for four C8-D units.

 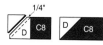

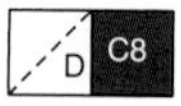

Figure 2
Stitch on the marked line.

Figure 3
Trim seam to 1/4" and press to the right side.

Step 7. Place a D square right sides together with the red side of one B8 unit; stitch on the line as shown in Figure 4. Trim seam to 1/4" and press to the right side to complete one B8-D unit as shown in Figure 5; repeat for four units.

 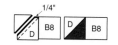

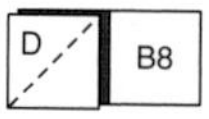

Figure 4
Place a D square on the red side of B8; stitch on the line.

Figure 5
Trim seam to 1/4" and press to the right side as shown to make a B8-D unit.

Step 8. Arrange the pieced units with E and A8 in rows as shown in Figure 6; join units to complete one red 8 block; repeat for eight blocks. Repeat Steps 6–8 to make six red 6 Star blocks.

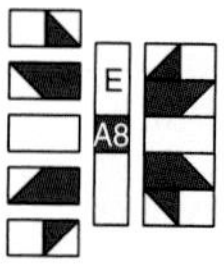

Figure 6
Arrange the pieced units with E and A8 in rows.

Making JOY Blocks

Step 1. Cut three 2 1/2" x 22" strips green tone-on-tone and one 4 1/2" by fabric width strip cream-on-cream print.

Step 2. Subcut one green strip into two 5 1/2" rectangles for F and one 1 1/2" rectangle for G.

Step 3. From the cream-on-cream print strip, cut three 1 1/2" squares for H and one 3 1/2" rectangle for J.

Step 4. Layer two H squares on the corners of F as shown in Figure 7; stitch and trim as in Step 6 for Star blocks to complete one F-H unit.

Step 5. Sew H to the end of G.

Step 6. To complete one J block, sew the G-H unit to J; add F and press. Sew an H-F unit to the G-H-F end to complete the block as shown in Figure 8; press.

Figure 7
Layer 2 H squares on the corners of F as shown; stitch and trim to complete 1 F-H unit.

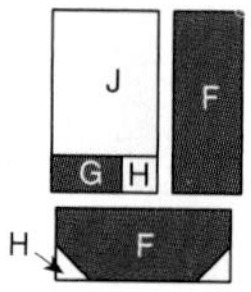

Figure 8
Sew the G-H unit to J; add F. Sew an H-F unit to the G-H-F end to complete the J block.

Step 7. From the second green strip cut in Step 1, cut two 5 1/2" F rectangles and two 3 1/2" rectangles for K.

Step 8. From the cream-on-cream print strip, cut one 1 1/2" x 3 1/2" rectangle for L and four 1 1/2" x 1 1/2" squares for H.

Step 9. Sew the H squares to F as in Step 4 to make two F-H units.

Step 10. To complete one O block, sew L between two K pieces; press. Sew an F-H unit to opposite ends of the pieced unit to complete one O block as shown in Figure 9.

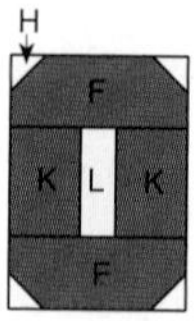

Figure 9
Sew K-L-K between 2 F-H units to complete the O block.

Step 11. From the last green strip cut in Step 1, cut two 5 1/2" F rectangles, one 4 1/2" rectangle for M and one 1 1/2" x 1 1/2" square for N.

Step 12. From the cream-on-cream print, cut two 1 1/2" x 3 1/2" rectangles for O and three 1 1/2" x 1 1/2" squares for H.

Step 13. Complete one F-H unit as in Step 4. Sew an H square to one corner of M as in Step 4 to complete one H-M unit as shown in Figure 10.

Step 14. Sew N to the end of one O.

Step 15. To complete one Y block, sew the O-N unit to the H-M unit; add O and then F referring to Figure 11. Sew the F-H unit to the O end to complete the Y block, again referring to Figure 11.

Figure 10
Sew an H square to 1 corner of M to complete 1 H-M unit as shown.

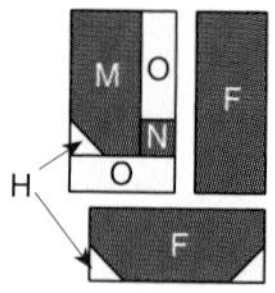

Figure 11
Sew the O-N unit to the H-M unit; add O and then F; sew the F-H unit to the O end to complete the Y block.

Quilt Assembly

Step 1. Cut four 1 1/2" by fabric width strips cream-on-cream print; subcut two of these strips into 5 1/2" segments for P. You will need 14 P pieces. Subcut the remaining strips into two 35 1/2" strips for Q.

Step 2. Join two red 6 and four red 8 Star blocks with five P strips to make a row as shown in Figure 12; repeat for two rows. Press seams toward P strips.

Step 3. Join two red 6 Star blocks with the J, O and Y blocks and four P strips to make a row as shown in Figure 13; press seams toward P strips.

Figure 12
Join 2 red 6 and 4 red 8
Star blocks with 5 P
strips to make a row.

Figure 13
Join 2 red 6 Star
blocks with the J, O
and Y blocks and 4 P
strips to make a row.

Step 4. Join the rows with the Q strips to complete the pieced center referring to Figure 14; press seams toward Q strips.

Step 5. Cut 12 strips green mottled 1 1/2" x 22". Join all strips on short ends to make one long strip. From this strip; cut four 17 1/2" (V) and four 35 1/2" (R) strips for borders.

Step 6. Cut four 3 1/2" x 3 1/2" squares red 6 for T. Cut the remaining red fabrics into 1 1/2" x 22" strips. Join the strips on the short ends to make one long strip. From this strip, cut two 17 1/2" (U) and two 35 1/2" (S) strips.

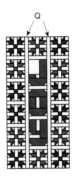

Figure 14
Join the rows with the
Q strips to complete
the pieced center.

Step 7. Sew a U strip between two V strips with right sides together along length; press seams in one direction. Repeat for two strips. Sew to the top and bottom of the pieced center; press seams toward strips.

Step 8. Sew an S strip between two R strips with right sides together along length; press seams in one direction. Repeat for two strips. Sew a T square to each end of each strip; sew to opposite long sides of the pieced center. Press seams toward strips to complete the pieced top.

Step 9. Prepare for quilting and quilt as desired referring to the General Instructions. *Note: The quilt shown was machine-quilted in a 1" grid in all cream-on-cream print areas using cream machine-quilting thread and in the ditch of border seams using thread to match fabrics.*

Step 10. Apply self-made or purchased binding referring to the General Instructions to finish. ❖

Sign of the Season
Placement Diagram
23" x 41"

Flaky Friends

By Sue Harvey

These pieced snowmen are welcome additions to your table from autumn until spring or, if you are a snowman collector, all year round!

Project Specifications

Skill Level: Beginner

Runner Size: 50" x 16"

Block Sizes: 4" x 4" and 8" x 12"

Number of Blocks: 4 and 2

Stocking Cap Snowman
8" x 12" Block

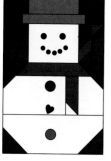

Top Hat Snowman
8" x 12" Block

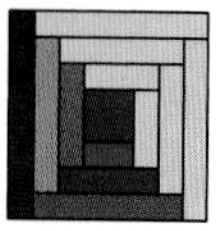

Reversed Log Cabin
4" x 4" Block

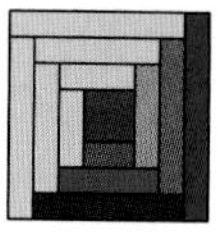

Log Cabin
4" x 4" Block

Materials

- 6 dark-colored fat quarters
- 1 fat quarter each black, red, green, gold and cream prints
- 2 fat quarters navy prints
- 1/2 yard tan print
- Batting 54" x 20"
- Backing 54" x 20"
- All-purpose thread to match fabrics
- Tan machine-quilting thread
- Clear nylon monofilament
- Basting spray
- 10 (3/8") assorted buttons
- 4 (1/2") assorted buttons
- 7 (5/8") assorted buttons
- Basic sewing tools and supplies, rotary cutter, mat and ruler

Instructions

Note: Fabrics are referred to as dark, navy, black, red, green, gold and cream throughout these instructions.

Making the Center Unit

Step 1. From each dark fat quarter and the red and green fat quarters, cut one strip 2 1/2" x 22".

Step 2. Join four 2 1/2"-wide strips along length with right sides together to make a strip set as shown in Figure 1; press seams in one direction. Repeat with remaining 2 1/2"-wide strips to make a second strip set.

Step 3. Cut two 2 1/2" segments from each strip set, again referring to Figure 1. Set aside remaining strip sets.

Step 4. Join the four segments to make the pieced center unit as shown in Figure 2; press seams in one direction. Set aside.

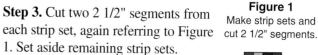

2 1/2"

Figure 1
Make strip sets and cut 2 1/2" segments.

Figure 2
Join segments to make the pieced center unit.

Making the Log Cabin Blocks

Step 1. From each dark fat quarter and the green fat quarter, cut one strip 1" x 22". Subcut the strips into the following segments: four 1" x 1 1/2" for D1, eight 1" x 2 1/2" for D2, eight 1" x 3 1/2" for D3 and four 1" x 4 1/2" for D4.

Step 2. Cut one strip 1 1/2" x 22" from the red fat quarter; subcut into four 1 1/2" square segments for R.

Step 3. Cut two strips 1" by fabric width tan print; subcut into eight segments each 1" x 2" for T1, 1" x 3" for T2 and 1" x 4" for T3.

Step 4. To piece one Log Cabin block, sew D1 to R; press seam toward D1. Sew T1 to the pieced unit as shown in Figure 3; press seam toward T1. Sew a second T1 to the pieced unit as shown in Figure 4; press seam toward T1. Sew D2 to the pieced unit as shown in Figure 5; press seam toward D2.

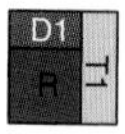

Figure 3
Sew T1 to the pieced unit.

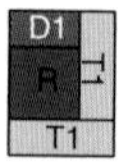

Figure 4
Sew a second T1 to the pieced unit.

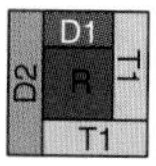

Figure 5
Sew D2 to the pieced unit.

Step 5. Continue adding segments around the pieced

unit until there are three rows on each side of R to complete the block as shown in Figure 6; press seams toward the last segment added. Repeat for two blocks.

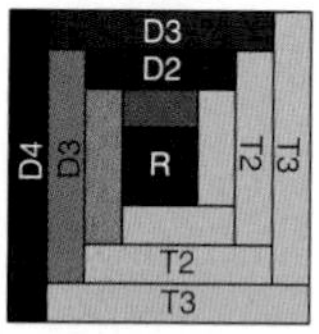

Figure 6
Complete 1 Log
Cabin block.

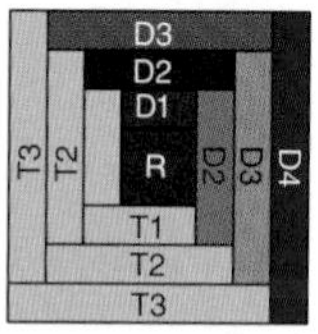

Figure 7
Complete 1 Reversed
Log Cabin block.

Step 6. To piece one Reversed Log Cabin block, repeat Steps 4 and 5 referring to Figure 7 for positioning of segments. Repeat for two blocks.

Step 7. Join a Log Cabin block and a Reversed Log Cabin Block as shown in Figure 8; repeat. Sew a block strip to opposite sides of the pieced center unit referring to the Placement Diagram for positioning of strips.

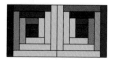

Figure 8
Join a Log Cabin block
and a Reversed Log
Cabin block to make a
block strip.

Making the Snowman Blocks

Step 1. Cut the pieces for the Top Hat Snowman and Stocking Cap Snowman blocks referring to the Cutting Chart.

Cutting Chart

Cream:	Navy:
3—1 1/2" x 1 1/2" for A	2—1" x 1 3/4" for J
2—1 7/8" x 5 3/4" for B	4—1 1/2" x 1 1/2" for K
1—2 1/2" x 8 1/2" for C	2—1 1/2" x 2 1/2" for L
1—2 1/2" x 3 1/2" for D	1—1 1/2" x 3 1/2" for M
2—3 1/2" x 4 1/2" for E	2—2" x 2 1/2" for N
1—3 1/2" x 5 1/2" for F	9—2 1/2" x 2 1/2" for O
1—3 1/2" x 8 1/2" for G	2—2 1/2" x 3 1/2" for P
1—5 1/4" x 5 1/4" for H	1—2 1/2" x 5 1/2" for Q
Red:	Green:
3—1 1/2" x 1 1/2" for R	1—1 1/4" x 5 1/2" for W
2—1 1/2" x 2 1/2" for S	2—1 3/8" x 3 3/8" for X
1—1 1/2" x 3 1/2" for T	1—1 3/8" x 7" for Y
1—1 1/2" x 8 1/2" for U	1—1 3/4" x 4 1/2" for Z
1—2 1/2" x 3 1/2" for V	

Step 2. Draw a diagonal line from corner to corner on the wrong side of one A, three K, nine O and three R pieces.

Step 3. To piece the Top Hat Snowman block, place A on one end of T as shown in Figure 9; stitch on the marked line, trim seam allowance to 1/4" and press A open as shown in Figure 10.

Figure 9
Place A on
1 end of T.

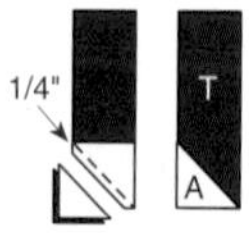

Figure 10
Stitch, trim seam
allowance and press.

Step 4. Sew D and F to opposite long sides of the A-T unit as shown in Figure 11; add G and U, again referring to Figure 11.

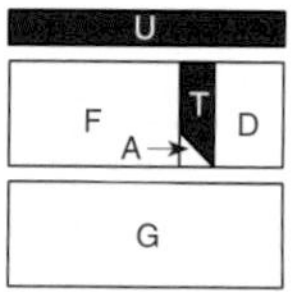

Figure 11
Sew D and F to A-T;
add G and U.

Figure 12
Complete the body
unit as shown.

Step 5. Place O right sides together on each corner of the pieced unit; stitch on the marked line, trim seam allowance and press O open to complete the body unit as shown in Figure 12.

Step 6. Place K on both ends of S, and R on one end of M; stitch, trim seam allowance and press to complete K-S and R-M units as shown in Figure 13. Sew the unmarked K square to K-S, again referring to Figure 13.

Figure 13
Complete K-S and R-M
units; add K to K-S.

Figure 14
Complete the
head unit.

Step 7. Join K-S and R-M units with E and P to complete the head unit as shown in Figure 14.

Step 8. Sew J to opposite short ends of Z; add W as shown in Figure 15. Sew N to each end of the pieced unit to complete the hat unit, again referring to Figure 15.

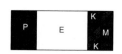

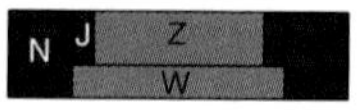

Figure 15
Complete the hat unit.

Step 9. Join the hat, head and body units to complete the block as shown in Figure 16.

Step 10. To piece the Stocking Cap Snowman block, cut remaining A squares in half on one diagonal to make triangles. Sew a triangle to one end of each X piece and both ends of Y as shown in Figure 17.

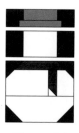

Figure 16
Join units to complete the
Top Hat Snowman block.

Figure 17
Sew A to X and Y.

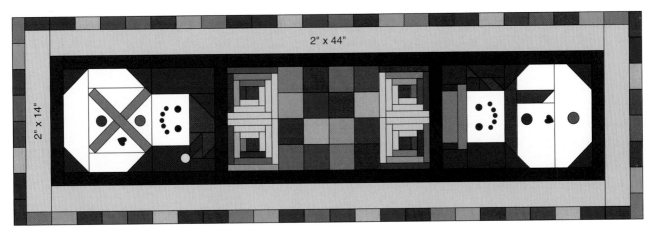

Flaky Friends
Placement Diagram
50" x 16"

Step 11. Cut the H square on both diagonals to make triangles. Sew H triangle to opposite sides of A-X as shown in Figure 18; repeat. Join the pieced units with A-Y, again referring to Figure 18.

Figure 18
Sew H to A-X;
join with A-Y.

Figure 19
Sew B and C to
the pieced unit.

Step 12. Sew B to opposite sides of the pieced unit and C to the bottom as shown in Figure 19.

Step 13. Place O right sides together on each corner of the pieced unit; stitch on the marked line, trim seam allowance and press O open to complete the body unit as shown in Figure 20.

Figure 20
Complete the body unit as shown.

Step 14. Place R on both ends of L, K on one end of S and O on one end of V; stitch, trim seam allowance and press to complete L-R, K-S and O-V units as shown in Figure 21.

Figure 21
Complete L-R, K-S
and O-V units.

Figure 22
Complete the
head unit.

Step 15. Join the pieced units with L as shown in Figure 22. Sew E to P and sew to the pieced unit, again referring to Figure 22; add Q to complete the head unit.

Step 16. Join the head and body units to complete the block as shown in Figure 23.

Completing the Runner

Step 1. Cut the following black print strips: four 1 1/2" x 10 1/2", four 1 1/2" x 12 1/2" and two 1 1/2" x 16 1/2".

Figure 23
Join units to complete the
Stocking Cap Snowman block.

Step 2. Sew a 12 1/2" strip to opposite long sides of each snowman block and a 16 1/2" strip to opposite long sides of the Log Cabin center unit; press seams toward strips.

Step 3. Sew a 10 1/2" strip to each end of the snowman blocks; press seams toward strips. Sew the bordered blocks to each end of the Log Cabin center unit referring to the Placement Diagram for positioning of blocks.

Step 4. Cut (and piece) two strips each 2 1/2" x 14 1/2" and 2 1/2" x 44 1/2" tan print. Sew the longer strips to opposite long sides and the shorter strips to the ends of the pieced center; press seams toward strips.

Step 5. Cut eight 1 1/2" segments each from the strip sets set aside in Making the Center Unit.

Step 6. Join three segments of each set on short ends to make a strip as shown in Figure 24; sew to opposite sides of the bordered center.

Step 7. Join one segment of each set on short ends to make a strip, again referring to Figure 24; sew to the ends of the bordered center to complete the top.

Figure 24
Join segments to make side and end border strips.

Continued on page 56

Christmas Keepsake Stocking

By Chris Malone

Three gift-shaped pockets provide added space for Christmas goodies.

Project Specifications

Skill Level: Beginner

Stocking Size: 9 1/2" x 15 3/4"

Materials

- 5–8 assorted red print fat quarters
- 1 fat quarter cream-with-gold metallic
- 1/2 yard quilter's fleece
- Red and ecru all-purpose thread
- Gold metallic fine braid (No. 8)
- 1 1/4 yards ecru twisted-cord piping with 1/2" tape
- 1 3/4 yards (3/8"-wide) wire-edged metallic red-and-gold ribbon
- Seam sealant
- Fabric glue (optional)
- Basic sewing tools and supplies, rotary cutter, mat and ruler, and zipper foot

Instructions

Step 1. Prepare template for stocking piece using pattern given, adding 1/2" all around pattern for seam allowance. Cut as directed on the pattern, cutting one fleece stocking piece 1" larger all around than the template.

Step 2. Cut a five-sided piece from one red print fat quarter about 5" across for piece 1; lay this piece right side up on the approximate center of the larger fleece stocking shape as shown in Figure 1.

Figure 1
Lay piece 1 right side up on the approximate center of the fleece stocking shape.

Figure 2
Lay piece 2 right sides together with piece 1 on the approximate same-size edge.

Step 3. From a second red print, cut a scrap large enough to cover one edge of the first piece; lay the piece right sides together with piece 1 on the approximate same-size edge as shown in Figure 2. Stitch along edge to attach to the fleece foundation piece. Trim seam allowance to 1/8"; fold the piece to the right side and press.

Step 4. Continue to cut pieces from the assorted red prints, cutting each piece large enough to cover the edge of the center piece and its adjacent pieces. Continue to stitch the pieces, creating new angles, until the entire fleece foundation piece is covered.

Step 5. Use pattern to cut stocking front from the patchwork/fleece layers. Stitch around outside edge 3/8" to hold layers together; trim fleece close to stitching.

Step 6. Draw three 3" x 3" squares on the wrong side of the cream-with-gold metallic, leaving at least 1/2" between squares.

Step 7. Layer the marked fabric over another same-size piece of cream-with-gold metallic with right sides together. Cut a piece of quilter's fleece this same size and place under the layers.

Step 8. Sew all around each square on the drawn lines; cut out 1/4" from stitched lines. Trim fleece close to stitching and clip corners.

Step 9. Cut a slash through one layer only of the fabric layer; turn right side out through the slash. Press seams flat; whipstitch opening closed.

Step 10. Arrange the squares on the stocking front referring to the Placement Diagram for positioning.

Step 11. Using 1 strand of gold metallic fine braid, blanket-stitch around three sides of each square to attach, leaving top edge open.

Step 12. Pin stocking back, right side up, on the remaining piece of fleece; stitch 3/8" all around. Trim fleece close to stitching.

Step 13. Pin piping to stocking front with raw edge of piping even with raw edge of stocking; clip curves as necessary.

Step 14. Using a zipper foot, machine-baste as close to piping as possible.

Step 15. With right sides together and leaving top edge open, sew stocking front and back together using a 1/2" seam allowance. Repeat with the two lining pieces; trim seams and clip curves. Turn stocking right side out; do not turn lining.

Step 16. Press a 1/2" hem to the inside on the top edge of the stocking and lining units. Insert lining inside stocking with wrong sides together; pin top edges.

Step 17. Cut a 1 1/2" x 4" strip from any red print. With right sides together, fold in half along length; sew along length with a 1/4" seam. Trim seam to 1/8"; turn right side out to make hanger.

Step 18. Fold hanger in a loop with raw edges overlapping at bottom; slip loop between lining and stocking at back edge beside the seam as shown in Figure 3; pin in place with about 1 1/4" of loop extending above top of stocking.

Figure 3
Place loop between lining and stocking at back edge seam.

Step 19. Slipstitch lining to stocking along top edge, catching hanger firmly in stitching.

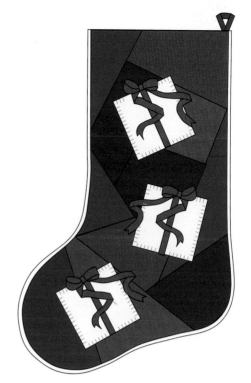

Christmas Keepsake Stocking
Placement Diagram
9 1/2" x 15 3/4"

Step 20. Cut three 3 1/4" lengths 3/8"-wide ribbon. Apply seam sealant to cut ends and let dry. Glue or tack each ribbon to the center of each pocket, starting at bottom and folding 1/4" end of ribbon over top edge of pocket.

Step 21. Cut remaining ribbon into three equal lengths; tie each in a bow. Cut ends in a V; apply seam sealant. Glue or tack a bow center to top of each pocket; fold and loop ends as desired. ❖

Flaky Friends
Continued from page 53

Step 8. Spray one side of the batting with basting spray; place backing piece on sprayed side and smooth. Repeat with completed top on remaining side of batting.

Step 9. Hand- or machine-quilt as desired. ***Note:** The sample shown was machine-quilted in the ditch of seams in the snowman blocks using clear nylon monofilament and 1/4" from seams in the borders using tan machine-quilting thread.*

Step 10. Trim edges even. Cut seven strips navy 2 1/4" x 22". Join strips on short ends; press in half along length with wrong sides together to make a binding strip. Bind edges of runner reffering to General Instructions.

Step 11. Sew two 1/2" buttons on each snowman for eyes, five 3/8" on each for mouth, three 5/8" on each for buttons and one 5/8" on the Stocking Cap Snowman for pompom on cap using tan machine-quilting thread and referring to the Placement Diagram for positioning. ❖

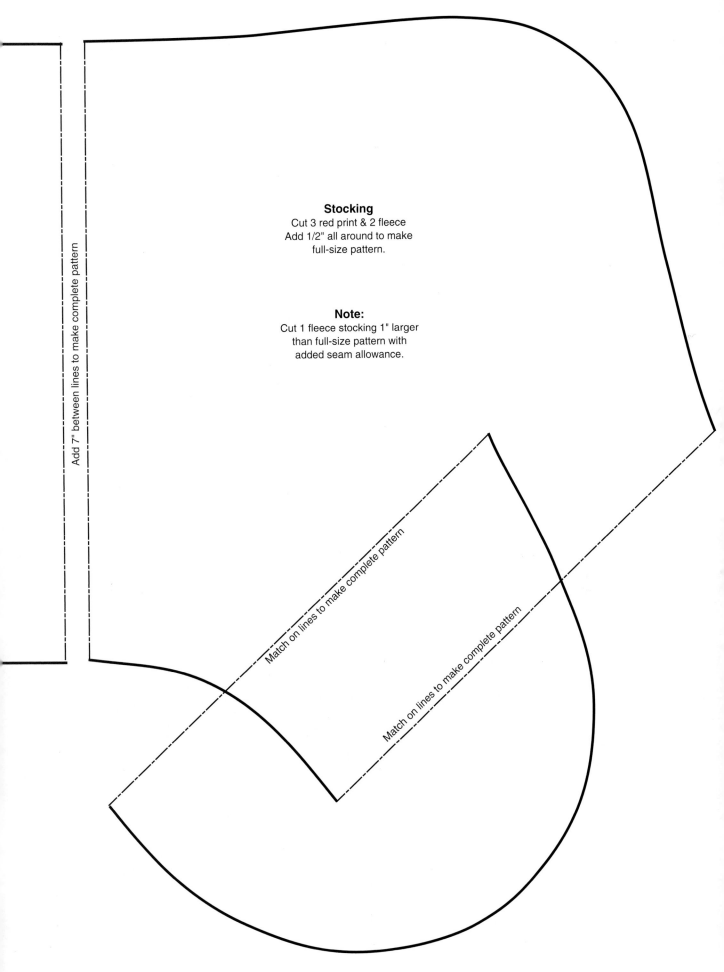

Stocking
Cut 3 red print & 2 fleece
Add 1/2" all around to make
full-size pattern.

Note:
Cut 1 fleece stocking 1" larger
than full-size pattern with
added seam allowance.

Add 7" between lines to make complete pattern

Match on lines to make complete pattern

Match on lines to make complete pattern

One-Color Quilting

Golds, yellows, reds and blues are colors that will shine as you stitch these quilts and projects created with fat quarters from just one color family.

By the Seashore

By Holly Daniels

The colors of the ocean combine with the Storm at Sea pattern to make a lovely monochromatic quilt.

Project Notes

All the fabrics used in this quilt are blue or aqua. Choose a variety of light and dark fabrics to provide contrast in the blocks. Maintain a scrappy look by using pieces of each fat quarter in each block.

Project Specifications

Skill Level: Beginner

Quilt Size: 98" x 98"

Block Sizes: 16" x 16"

Number of Blocks: 25

Ocean Waves
16" x 16" Block

Storm at Sea
16" x 16" Block

Materials

- 18 light blue/aqua fat quarters
- 21 dark blue/aqua fat quarters
- 2 1/2 yards blue mottled
- Batting 102" x 102"
- Backing 102" x 102"
- 11 1/3 yards self-made or purchased binding
- All-purpose thread to match fabrics
  - Clear nylon monofilament
  - Basic sewing tools and supplies, rotary cutter, mat and ruler

Instructions

Ocean Waves Blocks

Step 1. Cut 13 squares light blue/aqua 6 1/8" x 6 1/8" for A.

Step 2. Cut 26 squares dark blue/aqua 4 7/8" x 4 7/8".

Cut each square in half on one diagonal to make B triangles; you will need 52 B triangles.

Step 3. Cut 45 strips each 2 7/8" x 21" light (C) and dark (D) blue/aqua fabrics.

Step 4. Layer one C and D strip with right sides together; press. Subcut strips into 2 7/8" square segments to make seven squares per strip; you will need 312 layered squares. Cut 52 squares on one diagonal through both layers to make 104 each light (C) and dark (D) triangles; set aside.

Step 5. Draw a line across the diagonal on the light square of the remaining 260 layered squares. Sew 1/4" on each side of the drawn line as shown in Figure 1; cut along the line and press triangles to the right side for 520 C-D units.

Figure 1
Sew 1/4" on each side of the drawn line; cut along the line and press triangles to the right side for C-D units.

Step 6. Sew two C triangles to a C-D unit as shown in Figure 2; repeat for 52 C-C-D units. Press seams toward C triangles.

Step 7. Sew a C-C-D unit to each side of A to complete a block center referring to Figure 3; press seams toward A. Repeat for 13 block center units.

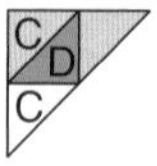

Figure 2
Sew 2 C triangles to a C-D unit.

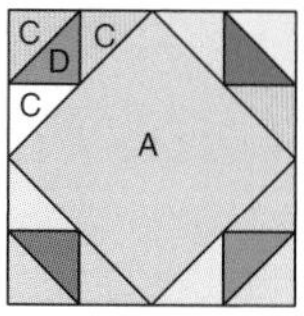

Figure 3
Sew a C-C-D unit to each side of A to complete a block center.

Figure 4
Sew 2 D triangles to a C-D unit. Add B.

Step 8. Sew two D triangles to a C-D unit as shown in Figure 4; repeat for 52 D-C-D units. Press seams toward D. Add B to each unit to complete 52 corner units, again referring to Figure 4. Press seams toward B.

Step 9. Join eight C-D units to make a side unit as shown in Figure 5; repeat for 52 side units.

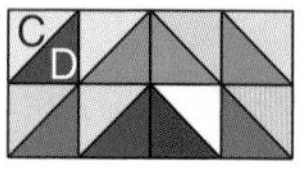

Figure 5
Join 8 C-D units to make a side unit.

Step 10. Sew a side unit to opposite sides of a center unit as shown in Figure 6; press seams toward side units.

Step 11. Sew a corner unit to opposite ends of two side units as shown in Figure 7; press seams toward side units.

Figure 6
Sew a side unit to opposite sides of a center unit.

Sew to opposite sides of the center/side unit to complete one Ocean Waves block as shown in Figure 8; press seams toward side/corner units. Repeat for 13 blocks.

Figure 7
Sew a corner unit to opposite ends of 2 side units.

Figure 8
Join units to complete 1 Ocean Waves block.

Storm at Sea Blocks

Step 1. Cut 12 squares dark blue/aqua 4 1/2" x 4 1/2" for E.

Step 2. Cut 24 squares 3 3/4" x 3 3/4" light blue/aqua; cut each square on one diagonal to make F triangles. You will need 48 F pieces.

Step 3. Sew F to each side of E as shown in Figure 9; press seams toward F. Repeat for 12 E-F units; trim each unit to 6 3/4" x 6 3/4".

Step 4. Cut 24 squares 4 7/8" x 4 7/8" dark blue/aqua; cut each square in half on one diagonal for G.

Step 5. Sew G to each side of an E-F unit as shown in Figure 10; press seams toward G. Repeat for 12 E-F-G units; trim each unit to 8 1/2" x 8 1/2".

Figure 9
Sew F to each
side of E.

Figure 10
Sew G to each
side of an E-F unit.

Step 6. Cut 48 squares 3 3/8" x 3 3/8" light blue/aqua for H.

Step 7. Cut 96 squares dark blue/aqua 2 7/8" x 2 7/8"; cut each square on one diagonal to make 192 J triangles.

Step 8. Sew J to each side of H as shown in Figure 11; repeat for 48 H-J units. Press seams toward J.

Step 9. Prepare templates for pieces K and L using pattern pieces given; cut as directed on each piece.

Step 10. Sew L and LR to K as shown in Figure 12; repeat for 48 L-K units.

Step 11. To piece one block, sew an L-K unit to opposite sides of an E-F-G unit as shown in Figure 13; press seams away from center unit.

Figure 11
Sew J to each
side of H.

Figure 12
Sew L and LR to K.

Figure 13
Sew an L-K unit to
opposite sides of an
E-F-G unit.

Step 12. Sew an H-J unit to each end of two K-L units as shown in Figure 14. Sew these units to opposite sides of the previously pieced unit to complete one Storm at Sea block as shown in Figure 15; press seams away from center unit. Repeat for 12 blocks.

Figure 14
Sew an H-J unit to each
end of 2 K-L units.

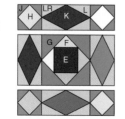
Figure 15
Join units to
complete 1 Storm
at Sea block.

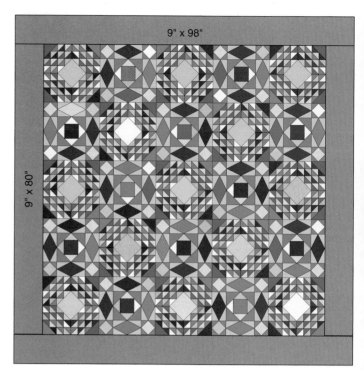
By the Seashore
Placement Diagram
98" x 98"

Completing the Quilt

Step 1. Join two Storm at Sea blocks with three Ocean Waves blocks to make a row as shown in Figure 16; repeat for three rows. Press seams in one direction.

Step 2. Join three Storm at Sea blocks with two Ocean Waves blocks to make a row, again referring to Figure 16; repeat for two rows. Press seams in one direction.

Step 3. Join the rows referring to the Placement Diagram for positioning; press seams in one direction.

Step 4. Cut and piece two strips each 9 1/2" x 80 1/2" and 9 1/2" x 98 1/2" blue mottled. Sew the shorter strips to opposite sides and longer strips to the top and bottom of the pieced center; press seams toward strips.

Step 5. Prepare for quilting and quilt as desired referring to the General Instructions. *Note: The quilt shown was machine-quilted in a meandering design using clear nylon monofilament in the top of the machine and all-purpose thread in the bobbin.*

Step 6. Apply self-made or purchased binding referring to the General Instructions to finish. ❖

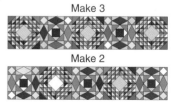
Make 3

Make 2

Figure 16
Join blocks to make rows as shown.

Patterns continued on page 65

Hearts Afloat

By Sandra L. Hatch

Shades of pink create the pieced hearts floating in this soft runner.

Project Specifications

Skill Level: Beginner

Runner Size: Approximately
48 1/2" x 18 1/2"

Block Size: 10" x 10"

Number of Blocks: 3

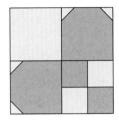

Hearts Afloat
10" x 10" Block

Materials

- 4 pink print fat quarters
- 2 fat quarters white-with-pink print or 1/2 yard
- Backing 52" x 22"
- Batting 52" x 22"
- White all-purpose thread
- Pink hand-quilting thread
- Clear nylon monofilament
- Basic sewing tools and supplies, rotary cutter, mat and ruler, and zipper foot

Instructions

Step 1. Cut one strip each pink print and three strips white-with-pink print 3" x 22".

Step 2. Sew a pink print strip to a white-with-pink print strip with right sides together along length; press seams toward darker fabric. Repeat for three strip sets.

Step 3. Subcut each strip set into 3" segments as shown in Figure 1; you will need two segments of each combination.

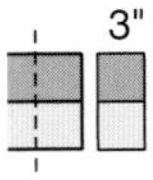

Figure 1
Subcut each strip set into 3" segments.

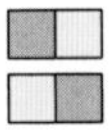

Figure 2
Join 2 same-fabric segments to make a Four-Patch unit.

Step 4. Join two same-fabric segments to make a Four-Patch unit as shown in Figure 2; repeat for three units. Press seams in one direction.

Step 5. Cut three white-with-pink print and two each pink print squares 6" x 6" for A.

Step 6. Cut one 1 3/4" x 22" strip white-with-pink print; subcut into 1 3/4" square segments for B. You will need 12 B squares. Draw a diagonal line from corner to corner on the wrong side of each B square.

Step 7. Place one B square right sides together with one pink print A square as shown in Figure 3; stitch on drawn line. Repeat on an adjacent corner, again referring to Figure 3.

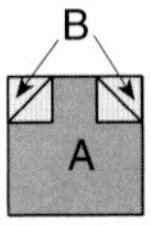

Step 8. Trim seams to 1/4" beyond stitching line and press B to the right side to complete an A-B unit referring to Figure 4; repeat for six A-B units.

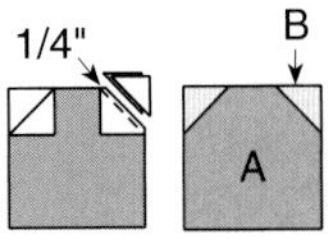

Figure 3
Place 1 B square right sides together with 1 A square.

Figure 4
Trim seams to 1/4" beyond stitching line and press B to the right side to complete an A-B unit.

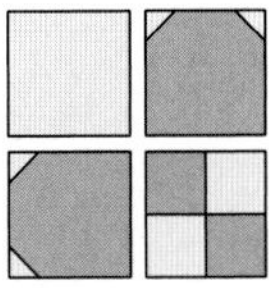

Figure 5
Join 2 same-fabric A-B units with 1 A and 1 Four-Patch unit to complete 1 Hearts Afloat block.

Step 9. Join two same-fabric A-B units with one white-with-pink print A and one same-fabric Four-Patch unit to complete one Hearts Afloat block as shown in Figure 5; repeat for three blocks. Press seams in one direction.

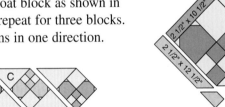

Figure 6
Sew C triangles to the pieced blocks.

Figure 7
Sew strips to ends; trim even with sides as shown.

Step 10. Cut one 15 3/8" x 15 3/8" square white-with-pink print; cut the square on both diagonals to make C triangles.

Step 11. Sew C triangles to the pieced blocks as shown in Figure 6; press seams toward C. Join these pieced sections to complete the pieced center; press seams toward C.

Step 12. Cut two strips each 2 1/2" x 10 1/2" and 2 1/2" x 12 1/2" different

pink prints. Sew the shorter strips to one side of each end block as shown in Figure 7; sew the longer strips to the remaining sides. Press seams toward strips.

Step 13. Cut excess strip at an angle even with side edges, again referring to Figure 7.

Step 14. Cut four 2 1/2" x 22" strips different pink fabrics. Join two strips on short ends to make a long strip; repeat. Center seam of strips with center blocks and pin in place with right sides together. Stitch along length; press seams toward strips. Trim excess on ends of each strip even with angle of previous strip to complete the pieced top referring to Figure 8.

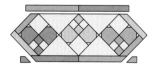

Figure 8
Trim excess on ends of
each strip even with angle of
previous strip to complete
the pieced top.

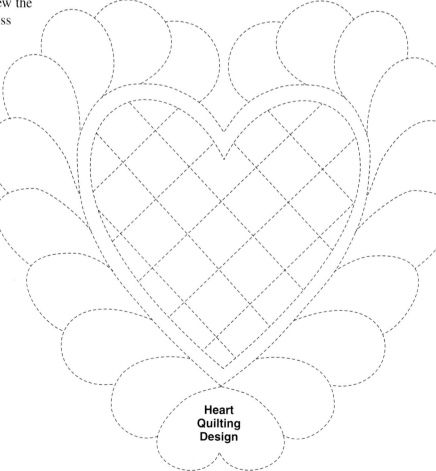

**Heart
Quilting
Design**

Step 15. Prepare for quilting and quilt as desired referring to the General Instructions. *Note: The quilt shown was hand-quilted using the quilting design given in the C triangles and in the ditch of some block seams and 1/4" inside seams using pink hand-quilting thread. Clear nylon monofilament was used in the top of the machine and all-purpose thread in the bobbin to quilt in the ditch of border seams and between blocks.*

Step 16. Cut five strips from one pink print 2 1/4" x 22"; join strips on short ends to make binding strip. Apply binding referring to the General Instructions to finish. ❖

Hearts Afloat
Placement Diagram
Approximately 48 1/2" x 18 1/2"

By the Seashore
Continued from page 62

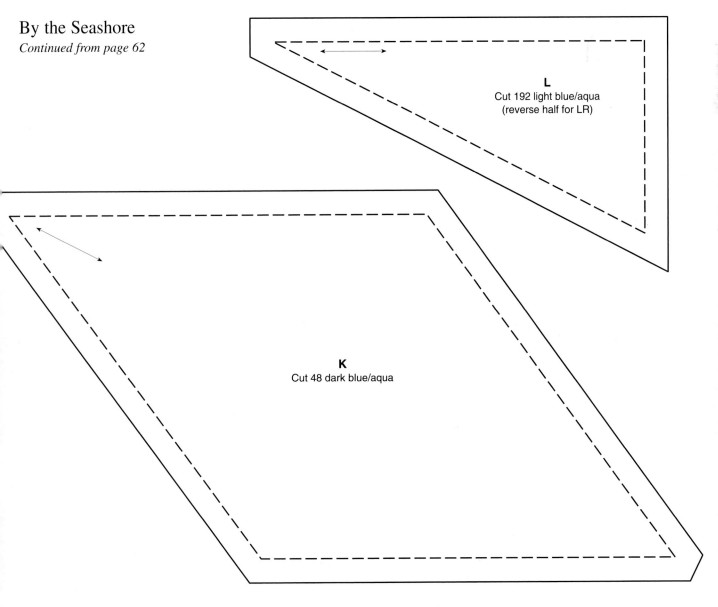

L
Cut 192 light blue/aqua
(reverse half for LR)

K
Cut 48 dark blue/aqua

Blue Floral Lap Quilt

By Barbara A. Clayton

Shades of blue yo-yo flowers combine with a Drunkard's Path block to make a pretty fabric flower garden.

Project Specifications

Skill Level: Intermediate
Quilt Size: 54" x 63"
Block Size: 9" x 9"
Number of Blocks: 10

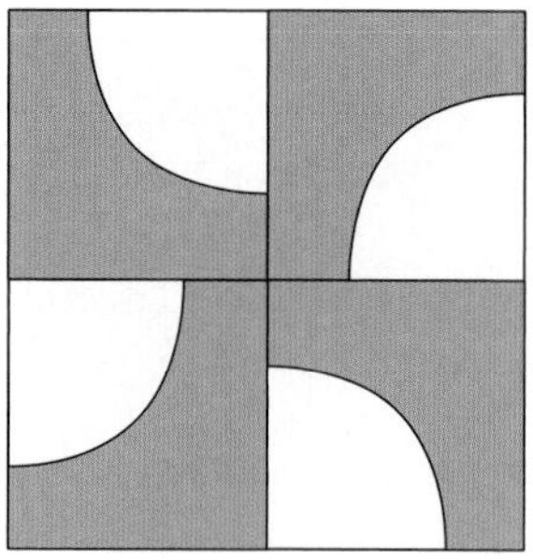

Materials

- 4 fat quarters navy prints
- 5 fat quarters light to medium blue prints for blocks
- 3/4 yard dark blue print
- 3/4 yard light blue print for border
- 3 1/2 yards cream-on-cream print
- Backing 58" x 67"
- Batting 58" x 67"
- All-purpose thread to match fabric
- Blue and white hand-quilting thread
- Clear nylon monofilament
- 2 1/2 yards medium-weight 22"-wide fusible interfacing
- 2 packages narrow navy double-fold bias tape
- Basic sewing tools and supplies, rotary cutter, mat and ruler, and lightweight cardboard

Drunkard's Path
9" x 9" Block

Instructions

Making Mock-Appliqué Blocks

Step 1. Prepare templates for A and B; cut as directed on each piece.

Step 2. Cut 60 squares cream-on-cream print 5" x 5". Pin the fusible interfacing A pieces to the squares with fusible side against the right side of the squares. Stitch the curved seam; trim away excess cream-on-cream print square and clip curve as shown in Figure 1. Turn right side out and hand-press curved edges smooth.

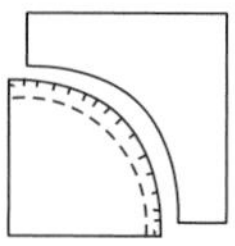

Figure 1
Trim away excess cream-on-cream print square and clip curve.

Step 3. Cut 60 squares light to medium blue prints 5" x 5". Pin the fused A pieces with the fusible side against the right side of each square as shown in Figure 2; iron to fuse in place. Repeat for 60 units.

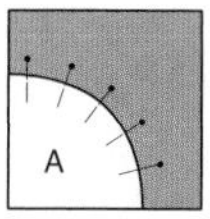

Figure 2
Pin the fused A pieces with the fusible side against the right side of each square.

Step 4. Using clear nylon monofilament in the top of the machine and all-purpose thread in the bobbin, machine-appliqué along edge of curve to secure in place.

Step 5. Trim away excess fabric from behind the cream-on-cream print area to reduce bulk.

Step 6. Join four same-fabric units to complete one Drunkard's Path block as shown in Figure 3; repeat for 10 blocks. Join two units to make a half block as shown in Figure 4; repeat for nine half blocks. You should have two units remaining. Set aside.

Figure 3
Join 4 same-fabric units to complete 1 Drunkard's Path block.

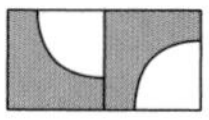

Figure 4
Join 2 units to make a half block.

Step 7. Cut four strips dark blue print 2 1/2" by fabric width; subcut into 2 1/2" square segments. You will need 60 squares.

Step 8. Pin the fusible interfacing B pieces to the squares with fusible side against the right side of the squares. Stitch the curved seam; trim away excess dark blue print square and clip curve as shown in Figure 5. Turn right side out and hand-press curved edges smooth.

Figure 5
Stitch the curved seam; trim away excess dark blue print square and clip curve.

Step 9. Cut 10 squares 9 1/2" x 9 1/2", nine 5" x 9 1/2" rectangles and two 5" x 5" squares cream-on-cream print. Pin the fused B pieces with the fusible side against the right side of each corner of each large square as shown in Figure 6; iron to fuse in place. Repeat on two corners of the rectangles and one corner of the small squares, again referring to Figure 6.

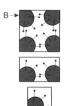

Figure 6
Pin the fused B pieces with the fusible side against the right side of each cream-on-cream print piece.

Step 10. Machine-appliqué in place as in Step 4; trim excess cream-on-cream print from beneath the B pieces to reduce bulk.

Piecing the Quilt Center

Step 1. Arrange and join two Drunkard's Path half and whole blocks with three large B squares to make a row as shown in Figure 7; repeat for two rows. Press seams in one direction.

Step 2. Arrange and join three whole Drunkard's Path blocks, two large B squares and two B rectangles to make a row as shown in Figure 8; repeat for two rows. Press seams in one direction.

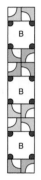
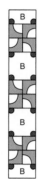

Figure 7
Arrange and join 2
Drunkard's Path half and
whole blocks with 3 large B
squares to make a row.

Figure 8
Arrange and join 3 whole
Drunkard's Path, 2 large B
squares and 2 B rectangles
to make a row.

Step 3. Join three half Drunkard's Path blocks, two B rectangles and two small B squares to make a side row as shown in Figure 9; press seams in one direction.

Step 4. Join two half Drunkard's Path blocks, three B rectangles and two A units to make a side row as shown in Figure 10; press seams in one direction.

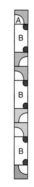

Figure 9
Join 3 half Drunkard's Path,
2 B rectangles and 2 small B
squares to make a side row.

Figure 10
Join 2 half Drunkard's Path
and 3 B rectangles and 2 A
units to make a side row.

Step 5. Join the rows referring to the Placement Diagram to complete the pieced center; press seams in one direction.

Blue Floral Lap Quilt
Placement Diagram
54" x 63"

Floral Appliqué

Step 1. Cut ten 12" lengths and twenty 5" lengths narrow navy double-fold bias tape for stems. ***Note:*** *You may make your own narrow bias tape using your favorite method. An extra fat quarter of navy solid or print is needed for the stem appliqué. A 1/4" bias bar helps to make creating the bias easier.*

Step 2. Trace the leaf design given onto lightweight cardboard; cut out. Trace shape onto the smooth side of the medium-weight fusible interfacing to make 120 leaves.

Step 3. Pin the traced interfacing with the glue side on the right side of navy fabrics; stitch on drawn lines through both layers. Cut out shapes, leaving a 1/4" seam allowance all around. Clip curves and trim points.

Step 4. Cut a small slit in the interfacing side of the stitched leaves; turn right side out, poking out points and smoothing curves. Transfer vein quilting lines to each leaf shape; set aside.

Step 5. Prepare template for yo-yo shape using pattern given; cut as directed on the pattern.

Step 6. Turn under 1/4" around edge of each circle and hand-stitch a line of gathering stitches 1/8" from edge all around; pull the thread tight and knot to gather the center of the circle to make a yo-yo as shown in Figure

11. Flatten each yo-yo between your fingers to form small round circles.

Step 7. Arrange one 12" and two 5" lengths bias tape on a large B square referring to Figure 12 for positioning. Machine-stitch close to edges using clear nylon monofilament in the top of the machine and all-purpose thread in the bobbin. Repeat for all large B squares.

Figure 11
Turn under 1/4" around edge of each circle and hand-stitch a line of stitching 1/8" from edge all around; pull the thread tight and knot to gather the center of the circle to make a yo-yo.

Step 8. Arrange two leaves on each 5" stem and eight leaves on each 12" stem as shown in Figure 13; fuse in place. Machine-stitch around each leaf as in Step 7.

Figure 12
Arrange one 12" and two 5" lengths bias tape on a large B square.

Figure 13
Arrange 2 leaves on each 5" stem and 8 leaves on each 12" stem.

Step 9. Sew a yo-yo to the end of each stem piece, extending yo-yo into the cream-on-cream print areas of the Drunkard's Path blocks referring to the Placement Diagram and stitching as in Step 7.

Finishing the Quilt

Step 1. Cut and piece two strips each 2" x 48 1/2" and 2" x 54 1/2" dark blue print. Sew the longer strips to opposite long sides and shorter strips to the top and bottom of the pieced center; press seams toward strips.

Step 2. Cut and piece two strips each 3 1/2" x 54 1/2" and 3 1/2" x 57 1/2" light blue print. Sew the longer strips to opposite long sides and shorter strips to the top and bottom of the pieced center; press seams toward strips.

Step 3. Trace the 9" scallop pattern line onto lightweight cardboard; use the 9" scallop pattern to trace six scallops on the top and bottom light blue print borders, lining the curve up with the edge of the quilt. Repeat with the 10"

scallop pattern line to trace six scallops on opposite long sides of the quilt top. Cut along traced lines to make scallop edges.

Step 4. Pin the quilt top right sides together with the prepared backing piece; stitch all around edges, using quilt front edge as a guide and leaving a 10" opening on one side. Place batting on the backing side; stitch again. Trim excess batting and backing even with edges of quilt top. Turn right side out through opening; hand-stitch opening closed.

Step 5. Quilt as desired by hand or machine to finish. *Note: The quilt shown was hand-quilted using white hand-quilting thread in the leaf veins and 1/4" from appliqué motifs using blue hand-quilting thread. Straight lines spaced 3/4" apart were hand-quilted with blue hand-quilting thread in the cream-on-cream print areas without appliqué as shown in Figure 14.* ❖

Figure 14
Quilt as shown.

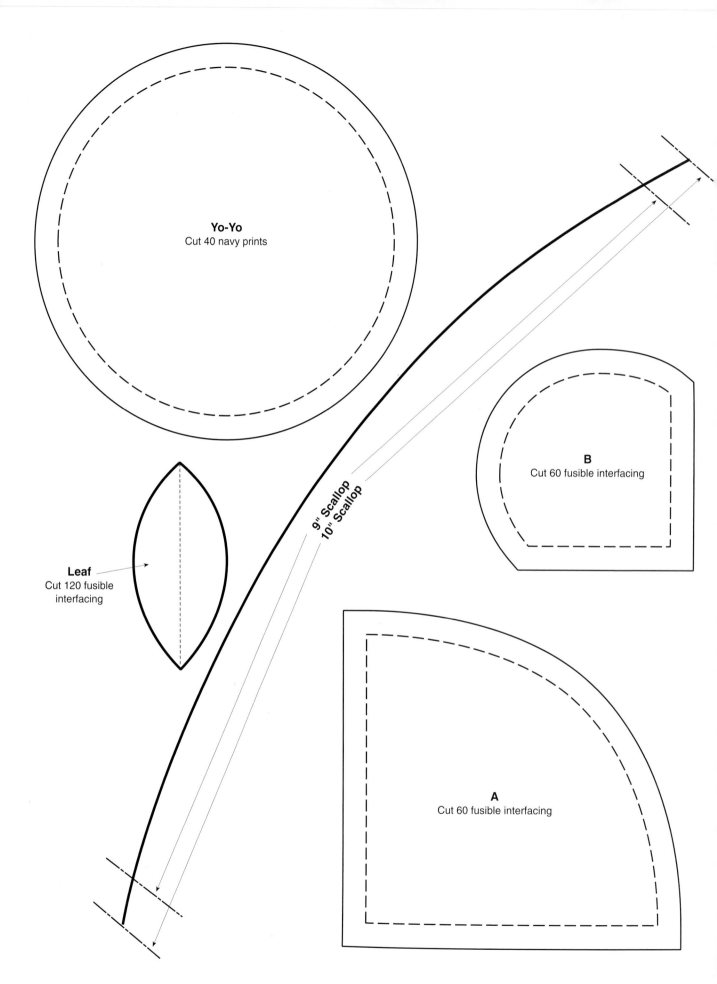

Yo-Yo
Cut 40 navy prints

Leaf
Cut 120 fusible
interfacing

9" Scallop
10" Scallop

B
Cut 60 fusible interfacing

A
Cut 60 fusible interfacing

Sunny Days

By Julie Weaver

The yellow and gold fabrics used in this wall quilt remind us of summer.

Project Specifications

Skill Level: Beginner

Quilt Size: 40" x 40"

Block Sizes: 12" x 12"

Number of Blocks: 4

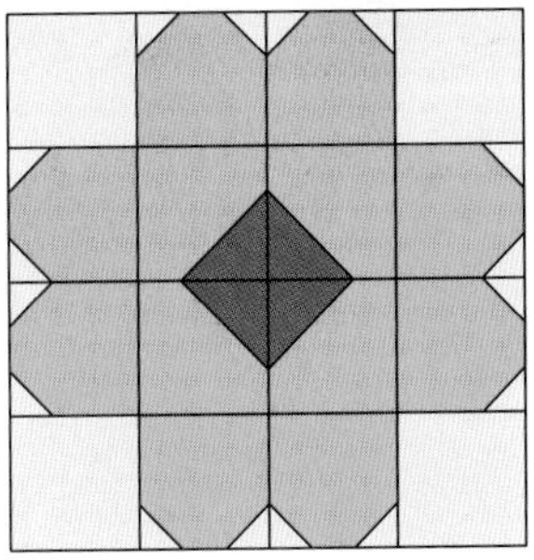

Materials

- 4 fat quarters yellow or gold tone-on-tones or mottleds
- 1/2 yard yellow tone-on-tone
- 1 yard dark gold mottled
- 3/4 yard yellow plaid
- Batting 44" x 44"
- Backing 44" x 44"
- Yellow all-purpose thread
- Brown/gold rayon twist thread
- Basic sewing tools and supplies, rotary cutter, mat and ruler

Sunny Days
12" x 12" Block

Instructions

Step 1. Cut two 3 1/2" x 22" strips each from the four yellow or gold fat quarters; subcut strips into 3 1/2" square segments for A. You will need 12 A squares from each fabric.

Step 2. Cut one 2 1/2" x 22" strip dark gold mottled; subcut into 2 1/2" square segments for B. You will need 16 B squares. Draw a diagonal line from corner to corner on the wrong side of each B square.

Step 3. Place a B square on an A square and stitch on marked line as shown in Figure 1; trim excess beyond the stitched line to 1/4" to make one A-B unit, again referring to Figure 1. Repeat for all A squares to make 16 A-B units; set aside. Press B to the right side.

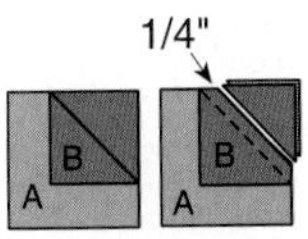

1/4"

Figure 1
Place a B square on an A square and stitch on marked line as shown; trim excess beyond the stitched line to 1/4" to make 1 A-B unit.

Step 4. Cut two 3 1/2" by fabric width strips yellow tone-on-tone; subcut into 3 1/2" square segments for C. You will need 16 C squares.

Step 5. Cut three 1 1/2" by fabric width strips yellow tone-on-tone; subcut into 1 1/2" square segments for D. You will need 64 D squares. Draw a diagonal line from corner to corner on the wrong side of each D square.

Step 6. Place a D square on one corner of an A square and stitch on marked line as shown in Figure 2; repeat on an adjacent corner. Trim excess 1/4" beyond the stitched line and press D to the right side to complete one A-D unit, again referring to Figure 2; repeat for 8 A-D units of each fabric.

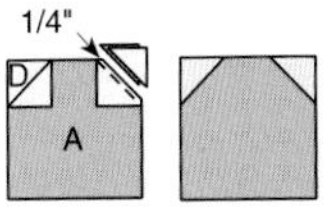

1/4"

Figure 2
Place a D square on 1 corner of an A square and stitch on marked line as shown; repeat on an adjacent corner. Trim excess 1/4" beyond the stitched line and press D to the right side to complete 1 A-D unit.

Step 7. To piece one block, join two C squares with two same-fabric A-D units to make a row as shown in Figure 3; repeat for two rows. Press seams toward C.

Make 2

Figure 3
Join 2 C squares with 2 same-fabric A-D units to make a row.

Make 2

Figure 4
Join 2 same-fabric A-D units with 2 same-fabric A-B units to make a row.

Step 8. Join two same-fabric A-D units with two same-fabric A-B units to make a row as shown in Figure 4; repeat for two rows. Press seams toward A-B units.

Step 9. Join the A-D-C rows with the A-D-B rows to complete one block as shown in Figure 5; press seams in one direction. Repeat for four blocks.

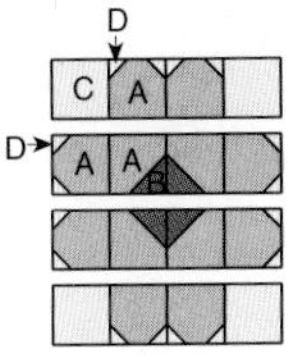

Step 10. Cut two 2" x 22" strips from each of the four yellow or gold fat quarters. Arrange the strips as desired for color order and sew together along length in that order; press seams in one direction.

Figure 5
Join the A-D-C rows with the A-D-B rows to complete 1 block.

Step 11. Subcut the strip set into 1 1/2" segments to make 1 1/2" x 12 1/2" E units as shown in Figure 6; you will need 12 E units.

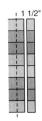

Figure 6
Subcut the strip set into 1 1/2" segments to make 1 1/2" x 12 1/2" E units.

Step 12. Cut one 12 1/2" by fabric width strip dark gold mottled; subcut into 1" segments for F. You will need 24 F segments.

Step 13. Sew an F segment to opposite long sides of each E unit as shown in Figure 7; press seams toward E.

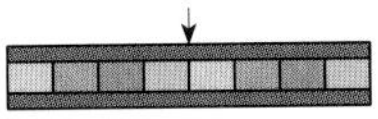

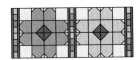

Figure 7
Sew an F segment to opposite long sides of each E unit.

Step 14. Join two blocks with three E-F units to make a block row as shown in Figure 8; repeat for two block rows. Press seams toward E-F units.

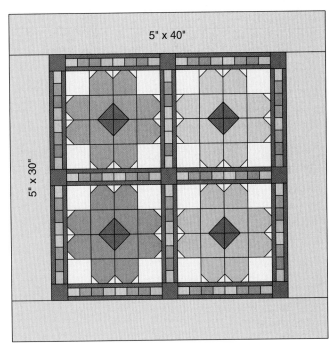

Figure 8
Join 2 blocks with 3 E-F units to make a block row.

Step 15. Cut nine 2 1/2" x 2 1/2" squares dark gold mottled for G.

Step 16. Join two E-F units with three G squares to make a row as shown in Figure 9; repeat for three rows. Press seams toward G.

Figure 9
Join 2 E-F units with 3 G squares to make a row.

Step 17. Join the E-F-G rows with the block rows to complete the pieced center as shown in Figure 10; press seams toward E-F-G rows.

Step 18. Cut two strips each 5 1/2" x 30 1/2" and 5 1/2" x 40 1/2" yellow plaid. Sew the shorter strips to opposite sides and longer strips to the top and bottom of the pieced center; press seams toward strips.

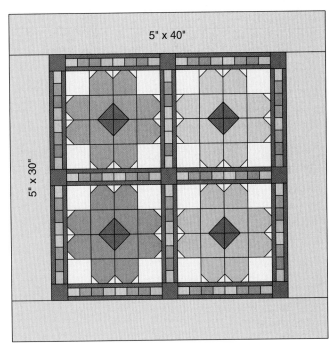

5" x 40"

5" x 30"

Sunny Days
Placement Diagram
40" x 40"

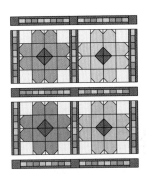

Figure 10
Join the E-F-G rows with the block rows to complete the pieced center.

Step 19. Prepare for quilting and quilt as desired referring to the General Instructions. *Note: The quilt shown was machine-quilted in the ditch of seams, 1/4" from some seams and then 1/2" from these seams using brown/ gold rayon twist thread.*

Step 20. Prepare 5 yards dark gold mottled binding and apply referring to the General Instructions to finish. ❖

Golden Pansies Table Mat

By Marian Shenk

Appliquéd flowers create this sunny-looking table mat.

Project Specifications

Skill Level: Intermediate

Mat Size: Approximately 40" x 18" (includes binding)

Materials

- 6" x 6" square gold solid
- 1 fat quarter yellow/green mottled
- 2 fat quarters dark gold print
- 4 fat quarters yellow to medium gold prints or mottleds
- 3/4 yard light yellow print
- Batting 44" x 22"
- Backing 44" x 22"
- All-purpose thread to match fabrics
- Cream hand-quilting thread
- Green and gold 6-strand embroidery floss
- Basic sewing tools and supplies, rotary cutter, mat and ruler

Instructions

Step 1. Prepare templates using pattern pieces given; cut as directed on each piece except for piece A.

Step 2. Cut a 4 3/4" x 4 3/4" square light yellow print.

Step 3. Cut one dark gold print fat quarter into 1" x 22" strips. Subcut one strip into two 4 3/4" and two 5 3/4" strips. Sew the shorter strips to opposite sides and longer strips to the top and bottom of the 4 3/4" x 4 3/4" square as shown in Figure 1; press seams toward strips.

Step 4. Cut four 1 1/2" x 22" strips from each yellow to medium gold fat quarters.

Step 5. Join one strip of each color along length with right sides together in a pleasing order; repeat for four identical strip sets. Press seams in one direction.

Figure 1
Sew the shorter strips to opposite sides and longer strips to the top and bottom of the 4 3/4" x 4 3/4" square.

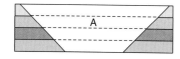

Figure 2
Place the A template on a strip.

Step 6. Place the A template on a strip as shown in Figure 2; cut. Repeat on each strip, placing A the same way on each strip.

Step 7. Sew an A strip to each side of the bordered square, mitering corner seams; press seams toward A and mitered seams in one direction.

Step 8. Cut two strips each 13 3/4" and 14 3/4" dark gold print from the 1"-wide strips cut in Step 3. Sew the shorter strips to opposite sides and longer strips to the top and bottom of the pieced center; press seams toward strips.

Step 9. Center and sew a B triangle to opposite ends of the pieced and appliquéd center. Cut four 13" strips dark gold print from the 1"-wide strips cut in Step 3. Sew a strip to one short side of each B triangle; sew a strip to the remaining side of B. Trim ends even with bordered center as shown in Figure 3; press seams toward strips.

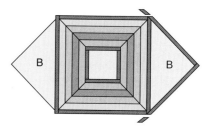

Figure 3
Sew a strip to each side of B; trim ends even with bordered center.

Step 10. Cut six strips 2" x 17" light yellow print. Sew a strip to opposite sides, trimming excess at each end at the same angle as the bordered B triangle as shown in Figure 4.

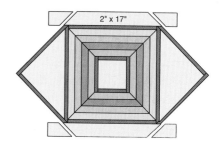

Figure 4
Sew a strip to opposite sides, trimming excess at each end at the same angle as the bordered B triangle.

Step 11. Sew two strips to each angled end, mitering corners at the end centers. Trim excess at side ends even with edge of the side border strips as shown in Figure 5.

Step 12. Turn under edges of each appliqué shape; baste to hold.

Step 13. Using all-purpose thread to match fabrics, hand-stitch one flower motif with eight leaves in the center of the stitched piece and four flower motifs and six leaves on each B triangle referring to the Placement Diagram for positioning of pieces.

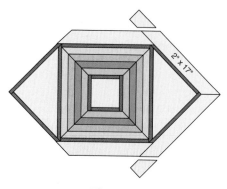

2" x 17"

Figure 5
Trim excess at side ends even with edge of the side border strips.

Step 14. Using 3 strands green embroidery floss, stem-stitch flower stems. Using 3 strands gold embroidery floss, buttonhole-stitch around flower center.

Step 15. Prepare for quilting and quilt as desired referring to the General Instructions. ***Note:*** *The quilt shown was hand-quilted in the ditch of seams, around each appliqué shape and in a cable design in the borders using cream hand-quilting thread.*

Step 16. Trim batting and backing even with the quilted top. Cut six strips dark gold print 1 1/2" x 22"; sew a strip to each edge of the table mat as in Steps 10 and 11 for light yellow print border using a 1/2" seam allowance.

Step 17. Turn under raw edge of dark gold print 1/4"; turn to the back-side of table mat. Hand-stitch in place to finish. ❖

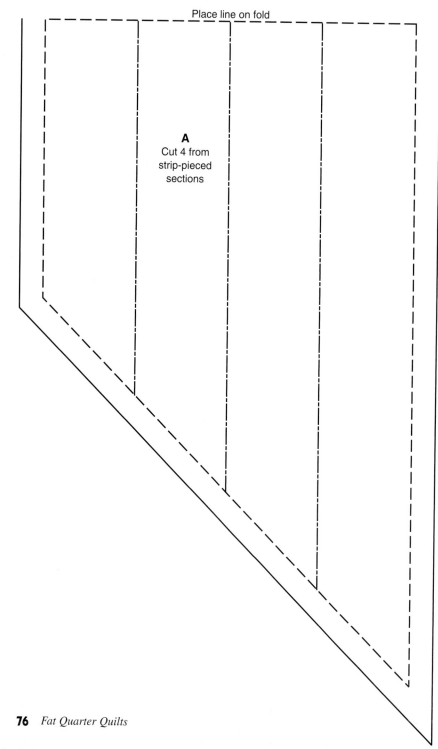

Place line on fold

A
Cut 4 from
strip-pieced
sections

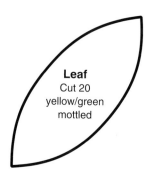

Leaf
Cut 20
yellow/green
mottled

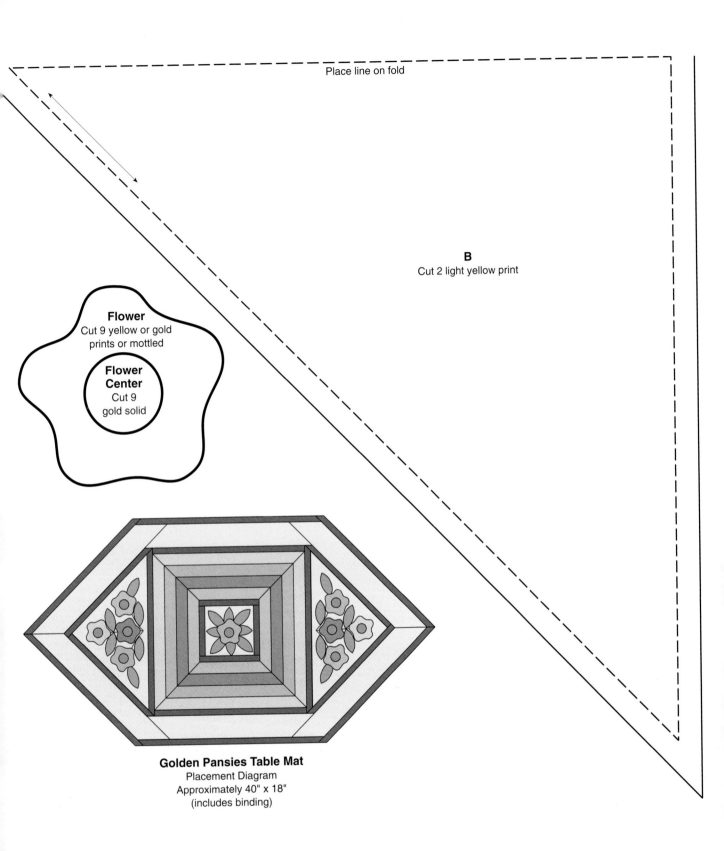

Place line on fold

B
Cut 2 light yellow print

Flower
Cut 9 yellow or gold
prints or mottled

**Flower
Center**
Cut 9
gold solid

Golden Pansies Table Mat
Placement Diagram
Approximately 40" x 18"
(includes binding)

Blue for You Kimono

By Willow Ann Sirch

Using one color in all its variations is a fun experiment that helps you appreciate the effect of subtle variations in hue and value.

Project Notes

This simple, patternless short kimono is loose-fitting, works up quickly and is a good weekend project. Machine sewing is recommended. The kimono is made here using traditional Japanese blue-on-white prints combined with hand-dyed blue cottons and blue Bali batiks. The project is made of four rectangles plus decoration, has no batting and is unquilted. Prewash and iron all fabrics before starting the project.

Use a rotary cutter to speed the process. Skip marking the patchwork strips and eyeball the 1/4" seam allowance as you sew. If you haven't tried this before, mark the 1/4" seam allowance on the sewing plate of your machine with a strip of masking tape. You'll be amazed at the accuracy of the results. To keep things simple, using 1/4" seams consistently throughout the project is recommended, rather than alternating between the 1/4" seams used in quiltmaking and the 3/8"–5/8" seams typically used to sew clothing. If you prefer larger seam allowances for the kimono fabric rectangles, you may add them in when determining your measurements.

The kimono edges feature sew-and-fold binding—just as if you were finishing off a quilt. If you've added binding clips to your notions stash, be sure to use them. They make the final hand-sewing of the binding edge much more pleasant, especially in a clothing project such as this in which there are more corners to turn than in a four-sided quilt.

Project Specifications

Skill Level: Intermediate

Project Size: Size varies

Materials

- 6–8 different medium-to-dark blue fat quarters for the decorative bars patchwork
- 6–8 different light-to-medium blue fat quarters for the decorative bars patchwork
- 6–8 different light blue fabric scraps at least 6" x 8"
- 1 fat quarter light blue "sky" fabric
- 3" x 7" scrap black print
- 2" x 2" scrap white solid
- 1 1/2 yards dark blue print fabric for unpieced sections
- 2 yards light blue print for lining
- 1/2 yard dark blue mottled for binding
- Dark blue all-purpose thread
- 1 dark blue 1" button
- One sheet of quilter's graph paper (optional)
- Basic sewing supplies and tools, rotary cutter, mat and ruler

Instructions

Making the Pattern

Step 1. Photocopy the kimono diagram given. ***Note:*** *Have a loose-fitting jacket or sweater on hand to guide you as you determine the correct measurements. Don't struggle with the measurements! Just round up to the nearest inch. Write in the measurements on the diagram so you have a frame of reference as you work.*

Kimono Back Pattern

Step 1. Take the vertical (up-and-down) measurement of the kimono back as shown in Figure 1. ***Note:*** *The vertical measurement should be approximately from the base of the neck to where you want the kimono to end (whether a little below the waist or down as far as your hips) plus 2".* Write in the vertical measurement on the kimono diagram.

Step 2. Take the horizontal (side-to-side) measurement. The total horizontal measurement should be from hip to hip plus 2". To figure the width of each kimono-back rectangle, subtract 6" (for the width of the center patchwork strip) from the total horizontal measurement, then divide by 2 as

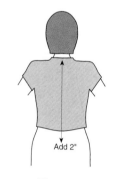

Figure 1
The vertical measurement should be approximately from the base of the neck to where you want the kimono to end (whether a little below the waist or down as far as your hips) plus 2".

shown in Figure 2. *Note: The horizontal measurement for the project sample was 22" plus 2" for a total of 24" across. Subtract 6" and that leaves 18". Divide 18 by 2 to get 9"—the size for each side rectangle without seam allowance .* Write the horizontal measurements on the kimono diagram.

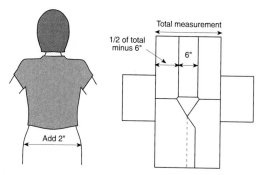

Figure 2
The total horizontal measurement should be from hip to hip plus 2". To figure the width of each kimono-back rectangle, subtract 6" (for the width of the center patchwork strip) from the total horizontal measurement, then divide by 2.

Kimono Front Pattern

Note: The kimono fronts overlap each other the width of the front center vertical strip.

Step 1. Write in the vertical measurement from the kimono back. *Note: This is the same for both back and front of the kimono.*

Step 2. The kimono front is made of two wide patchwork strips and four narrow plain fabric strips. To find the width of the narrow fabric strips, take the total horizontal measurement from the kimono back (hip-to-hip plus 2"), subtract 12" (for the two patchwork strips) from the total horizontal measurement, then divide by 4 as shown in Figure 3. *Note: The horizontal measurement for the project sample was 22" plus 2" for a total of 24" across. Subtract 12" and that leaves 12". Divide 12" by 4 to get 3"—the size for each side rectangle without seam allowance.*

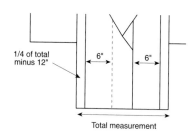

Figure 3
Take the total horizontal measurement from the kimono back (hip-to-hip plus 2"), subtract 12" (for the 2 patchwork strips) from the total horizontal measurement, then divide by 4.

Write this front measurement on the front edges and left front kimono diagram area. Multiply this measurement by 2; write this measurement on the right front kimono diagram area.

Kimono Sleeves Pattern

Note: Each sleeve is made of one rectangle folded over. The fold falls across the top of the sleeve. The end of the sleeve should fall approximately in the middle of your forearm—halfway between wrist and elbow. This is the sleeve length—also the horizontal measurement of the sleeve rectangle.

Step 1. To find the width of the narrow fabric strips for the sleeves, take the sleeve length and subtract 6" (for the center patchwork strip). Divide by 2 as shown in Figure 4. *Note: The total sleeve length on the sample project is 14". Subtract 6" and that leaves 8". Divide by 2 to get 4"—the size for each strip without seam allowance.* Write the sleeve length on the kimono diagram.

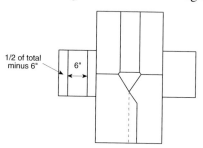

Figure 4
To find the width of the narrow sleeve strips, take the sleeve length and subtract 6" (for the center patchwork strip), then divide by 2.

Step 2. Find the vertical measurement of the sleeve which should allow the underarm of the sleeve to begin in the upper one-third of the kimono. The looser you want the sleeve, the longer you should make the vertical measurement as shown in Figure 5. *Note: The unsewn folded sleeve on the sample was 12" long. When sewn, it falls in the upper one-third of the kimono body. It could, however, be as long as 18" which, when sewn, would make the underarm of the sleeve fall at about the midpoint of the kimono body for a wider, looser, true kimono sleeve.* Write the vertical measurement for the sleeve on the kimono diagram.

Figure 5
Several sleeve lengths may be chosen.

Making the Kimono

Step 1. From dark blue print, cut two rectangles for the kimono back, the four narrow strips for the kimono front, and the two narrow strips for each of the two sleeves, adding 1/2" to measurements on the diagram for seam allowance. Press and set aside; repeat for the lining fabric.

Step 2. To make the "bars" patchwork strips, fold the fat quarters along length and cut two or more 2 1/2" strips from each fabric for a total of 20–24 strips. *Note: Check the measurements of your fat quarters; they should be at least 18" x 22".*

Step 3. Organize the strips in a pleasing color order. *Note: Avoid having two of the same strip next to each other.* Sew together along length with right sides together to make strip sets of six to eight strips each.

Step 4. Subcut the strip sets in 6 1/2" bar segments as shown in Figure 6; join the segments on the 6 1/2" sides to make a single long strip of patchwork to be cut to size as needed.

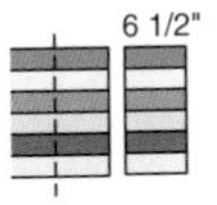

6 1/2"

Figure 6
Subcut the strip sets in 6 1/2" bar segments.

Step 5. To complete the mountain-scene square for the kimono back, cut a 4 1/2" x 10 1/2" rectangle from the "sky" fabric; set aside.

Step 6. Prepare templates for mountain and moon shapes using patterns given; cut as directed on each piece, adding a 1/4" seam allowance all around when cutting. Baste under the seam allowance on the top edge of the mountain and all around the moon; set aside.

Step 7. To make the bottom half of the mountain scene, cut short strips in random widths of 3/4" to 2" from the light blue fabric scraps. With right sides together, join two or three same-width strips on the short ends to make 12 1/2"-long strip sets as shown in Figure 7. Join the strip sets to make a rectangle approximately 6 1/2" x 12". Trim to make a 6 1/2" x 10 1/2" rectangle as shown in Figure 8.

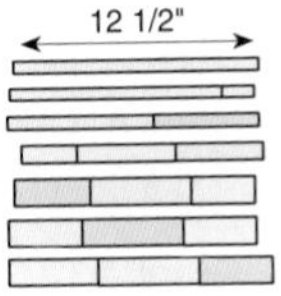

12 1/2"

Figure 7
Join 2 or 3 same-width strips on the short ends to make 12 1/2"-long strip sets.

10 1/2"

6 1/2"

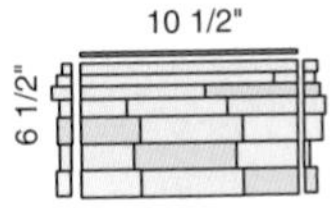

Figure 8
Trim to make a 6 1/2" x 10 1/2" rectangle.

Step 8. Position the mountain appliqué along the bottom of the sky fabric, referring to the Placement Diagram for positioning; appliqué in place. Repeat for the moon piece.

Step 9. With right sides together, sew the strip-pieced rectangle to the bottom of the appliquéd sky section to complete the mountain-scene square as shown in Figure 9.

Figure 9
Sew the strip-pieced rectangle to the bottom of the appliquéd sky section to complete the mountain-scene square.

Step 10. Cut a 10" x 10" sheet of paper. *Note: Quilter's graph paper works great for this.* Center and pin the mountain-scene square right side up on the paper square. The mountain scene should extend 1/4" beyond the edge of the paper all the way around. Press

the 1/4" seam allowance of the mountain scene down over the paper; set aside.

Step 11. Referring to the kimono diagram, cut a strip from the long bars strip set in the same vertical length as the kimono back, adding 1/2" to measurement on the diagram for seams. Sew one dark blue print kimono-back rectangle to each long side of the bars patchwork strip as shown in Figure 10; press seams away from pieced strip.

Figure 10
Sew 1 kimono back rectangle to each long side of the bars patchwork strip.

Step 12. Center the mountain-scene square at the base of the third strip from the top neck edge; baste in place. Hand-stitch in place all around. Trim excess pieced strip away from under the appliqué area, being careful not to cut through the outside square.

Step 13. Referring to the kimono diagram, cut two strips from the bars strip set in the same vertical length as kimono front, adding 1/2" for seams; stitch two dark blue print front pieces to each long side of each bar strip. Press seams away from pieced strip.

Step 14. Place each sewn strip right side up and lengthwise on a work surface. Make a 45-degree diagonal cut at the top of each front strip to make the neckline as shown in Figure 11; be sure to place the wider dark blue print at right front center.

Figure 11
Make a 45-degree diagonal cut in the top of each front strip to make the neckline.

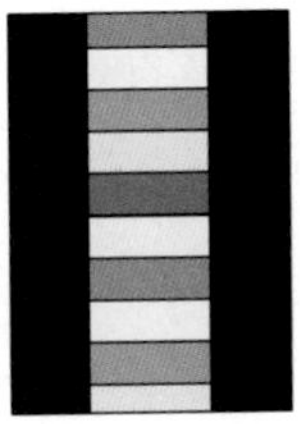

Figure 12
Stitch 2 sleeve pieces to each long side of each bar strip.

Step 15. Referring to the kimono diagram, cut two strips from the bars strip set in the same vertical lengths as kimono sleeves, adding 1/2" seam allowance. Stitch a dark blue print sleeve piece to each long side of each bar strip as shown in Figure 12; press seams away from pieced strip.

Step 16. Using the stitched units as pattern pieces, cut lining pieces from lining fabric.

Step 17. With right sides together, sew the kimono front to the kimono back along the shoulders; press seams open. Repeat for the kimono lining back and front.

Step 18. Fold the sleeve along the length to locate the center point (which will become the top of the sleeve); mark lightly. Line up this point with the shoulder seam that joins the kimono front and back. With right sides

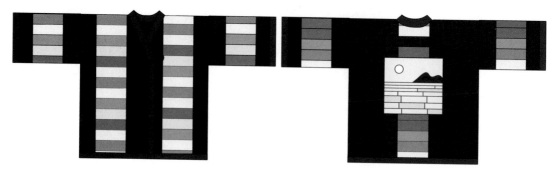

Blue for You Kimono
Placement Diagram
Size Varies

together sew sleeves to the kimono body. Repeat for the kimono lining sleeves, sewing them to the kimono body lining; press seams open.

Step 19. With right sides together, sew up the right side of the kimono, into the underarm and out along the bottom of the right sleeve as shown in Figure 13; press seams open. Repeat on the left side of the kimono. Repeat for the kimono lining. *Note: The outer part of the kimono and the lining are still separate.*

Figure 13
Sew up the right side of the kimono, into the underarm and out along the bottom of the right sleeve.

Figure 14
Trim the back neckline so it is slightly curved, cutting into the fabric back and lining approximately 1" as needed.

Step 20. Pin the wrong side of the kimono to the wrong side of the lining, matching all seams and edges. Trim the back neckline so it is slightly curved, cutting into the fabric back and lining approximately 1" as needed referring to Figure 14. Baste 1/8" from the outside edge all the way around.

Step 21. Cut two 4" by fabric width strips from the binding fabric to finish the bottom edge of each sleeve. Fold each strip in half along length with wrong sides together; press.

Step 22. Measure the finished size of the bottom edge of each sleeve; cut each binding strip this length plus 1/2". Stitch each strip together on short ends to make a tube.

Step 23. Turn under 1/4" along raw edge of each tube; press.

Step 24. Sew remaining raw edge of tube to the bottom edge of a sleeve with right sides together, matching seam allowance of tube with seam allowance of sleeve; press seam toward binding strips. Repeat for second sleeve.

Step 25. Fold each binding strip to the inside over stitched seam between sleeve and binding—the seam will be covered by the folded strip—to make a 1 3/4"-wide cuff. Hand-stitch in place on lining side to finish sleeves.

Step 26. Measure the distance around the kimono edges, not including the neck edge. Cut and piece a 2 1/2" strip this measurement plus 1/2".

Step 27. Fold under 1/4" along one long edge of the binding strip; press. Pin the raw edge of the binding strip to the raw edges of the kimono, starting and ending at the diagonal neck edges; stitch in place. Trim excess at ends even with kimono, if necessary.

Step 28. Turn the binding strip to the wrong side, covering seam on the inside, to make a 1"-wide finished binding; hand-stitch in place.

Step 29. Measure the distance around unfinished neck edge. Cut a piece of the remaining 4"-wide strip this length plus 1/2".

Step 30. Fold the strip with right sides together with pressed edge 1/4" below remaining raw edge as shown in Figure 15.

Figure 15
Fold the strip with right sides together with pressed edge 1/4" below remaining raw edge.

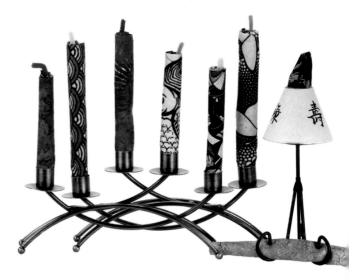

Step 31. Pin the right side raw edge of the neck binding strip to the right side of the neck edge; stitch all around stitch all around, overlapping beginning and end; turn the corners right side out; turn to the inside, enclosing seam, to make a 1"-wide binding strip. Adjust angled seam to create a continuous angle with the center front edge as necessary. Hand-stitch the binding to the inside neck edge, enclosing seam.

Step 32. Try on the finished kimono, overlapping top front edges. Mark the point where edges overlap for button placement.

Step 33. Cut a 1/2" x 4" piece of binding fabric. Fold in each long edge 1/8"; press. Fold strip with wrong sides together and stitch along open edge to make a loop. Hand-stitch the loop to the top backside edge of binding. Sew button in place as marked to finish. ❖

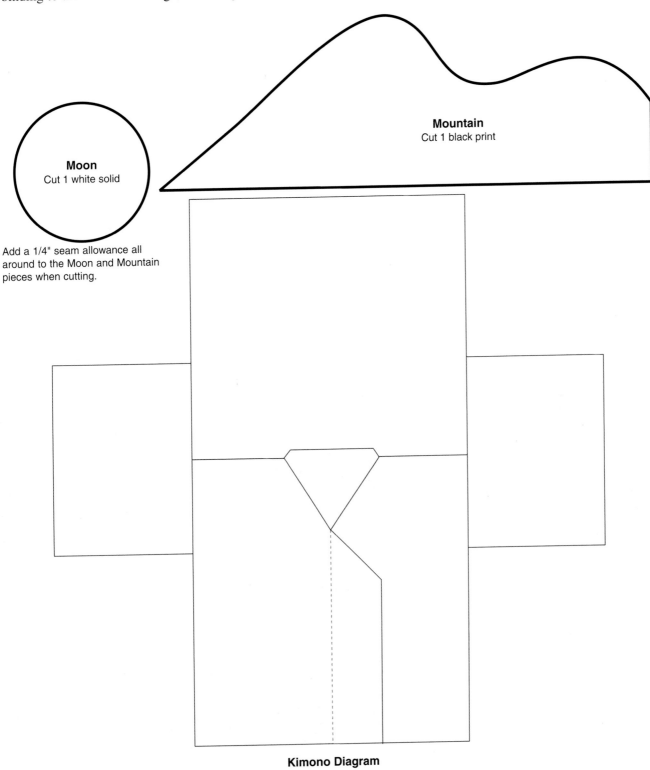

Moon
Cut 1 white solid

Mountain
Cut 1 black print

Add a 1/4" seam allowance all around to the Moon and Mountain pieces when cutting.

Kimono Diagram

Fat Quarter Classics

Stars, flags, houses and flying geese decorate these fat-quarter quilts and projects stitched from the classic patterns everyone loves to quilt and share.

Evergreen Lane

By Julie Weaver

Appliquéd Tree blocks combine with pieced House blocks to make this country quilt.

Project Specifications

Skill Level: Beginner

Quilt Size: 40" x 50"

Block Size: 9" x 7" and 4" x 7"

Number of Blocks: 10 House and 15 Tree

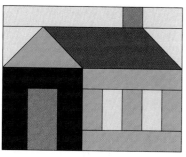

House
9" x 7" Block

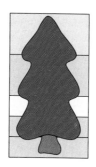

Tree
4" x 7" Block

Materials

- 1 fat quarter brown plaid
- 1 fat quarter brown check
- 2 fat quarters blue
- 2 fat quarters red
- 2 fat quarters gold/brown
- 4 fat quarters green
- 5 fat quarters cream/off-white
- 1 yard green tone-on-tone for borders and binding
- Backing 44" x 54"
- Batting 44" x 54"
- All-purpose thread to match fabrics
- Cream machine-quilting thread
- 2/3 yard fusible transfer web
- 3/4 yard fabric stabilizer
- Basic sewing tools and supplies, rotary cutter, mat and ruler

Instructions

Tree Blocks

Step 1. Cut twelve 1 1/2" x 22" strips cream/off-white; subcut strips into 4 1/2" segments for A as shown in Figure 1. You will need 45 A pieces.

Step 2. Cut eight 2 1/2" x 22" strips cream/off-white; subcut strips into 4 1/2" segments for B as shown in Figure 2. You will need 30 B pieces.

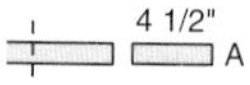

Figure 1
Subcut strips into 4 1/2"
segments for A.

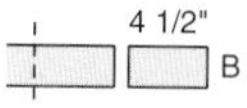

Figure 2
Subcut strips into 4 1/2"
segments for B.

Step 3. Join two B and three A pieces to make an A-B background block for tree appliqué as shown in Figure 3; repeat for 15 A-B blocks.

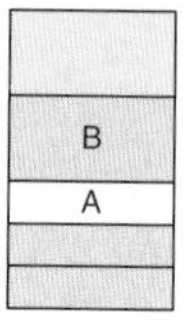

Step 4. Prepare templates for tree and tree trunk pieces. Trace 15 of each shape onto the paper side of the fusible transfer web; cut out shapes, leaving a margin around each one.

Figure 3
Join 2 B and 3 A
pieces to make an
A-B background block
for tree appliqué.

Step 5. Fuse tree shapes to the wrong side of two green fabrics, seven trees on one fabric and eight trees on another, and the trunk shapes to the wrong side of the brown check; cut out shapes on the traced lines. Remove paper backing.

Step 6. Arrange one tree and one tree trunk shape on an A-B background block, tucking the tree trunk under the tree referring to the pattern for placement; fuse in place.

Step 7. Cut a 4" x 7" piece fabric stabilizer; pin to the wrong side of the fused block. Machine-appliqué shapes in place using all-purpose thread to match fabrics and a narrow satin stitch. Remove fabric stabilizer. Repeat for 15 Tree blocks.

House Blocks

Note: Instructions are given to make one House block; you will need three each red and blue, and two each gold/brown and green houses. Reverse fabrics for front and peaks/side on one house of each color. One red and one blue house will be repeated.

Step 1. Cut three 1 1/2" x 2 1/2" rectangles for C, two 2 1/2" x 2 1/2" squares for D and one 1 1/2" x 6 1/2" rectangle for E from cream/off-white.

Step 2. Cut one 2 1/2" x 7 1/2" rectangle brown plaid for F (roof).

Step 3. Cut one 1 1/2" x 1 1/2" square for G (chimney) and one 2" x 3 1/2" rectangle for H (door) from brown check.

Step 4. Cut two 1 3/4" x 3 1/2" rectangles for J and 1 1/2" x 4 1/2" rectangles for K from one blue for house front.

Step 5. Cut one 2 1/2" x 4 1/2" rectangle for L, three 1 1/2" x 2 1/2" rectangles for M and two 1 1/2" x 5 1/2" rectangles for N from a second blue.

Step 6. Make a mark 2 1/2" from one corner along long edge of L. Draw a line from mark to corner on the wrong side of L as shown in Figure 4. To make the roof section, place L on the left end of F, again referring to Figure 4. Stitch on the marked line, trim seam to 1/4" and press L to the right side referring to Figure 5.

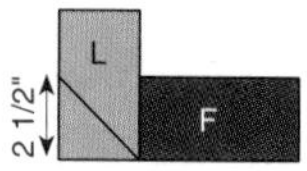

Figure 4
To make the roof section, place L on the left end of F.

Step 7. Draw a diagonal line from corner to corner on each D square. Lay a D square right sides together on the left side of L; stitch on marked line. Trim seam to 1/4"; press D to the right side referring to Figure 6.

Repeat with a second D on the remaining end of F referring to Figure 7 to complete the roof unit.

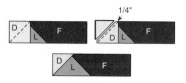
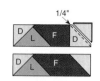

Figure 6
Lay a D square right sides together on the left side of L; stitch on marked line. Trim seam to 1/4"; press D to the right side.

Figure 7
Repeat with a second D on the remaining end of F to complete the roof unit.

Step 8. Join remaining pieces in units referring to Figure 8; join units to complete one House block, again referring to Figure 8.

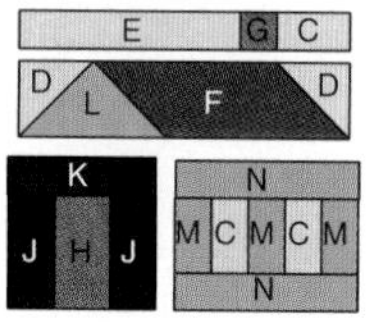

Figure 8
Join remaining pieces in units; join units to complete 1 House block.

Evergreen Lane
Placement Diagram
40" x 50"

Completing the Quilt

Step 1. Join two House blocks and three Tree blocks to make an X row as shown in Figure 9; repeat for three rows. Press seams toward House blocks.

Figure 9
Join 2 House blocks and 3 Tree
blocks to make an X row.

Step 2. Join two House blocks and three Tree blocks to make a Y row as shown in Figure 10; repeat for two rows. Press seams toward House blocks.

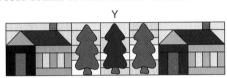

Figure 10
Join 2 House blocks and 3 Tree
blocks to make a Y row.

Step 3. Cut the remaining cream/off-white fat quarters into 1 3/4" by fabric width strips. Cut each strip in half to make approximate 10 1/2" lengths.

Step 4. Join strips as shown in Figure 11 to make a long strip; cut strip into four strips 30 1/2" long.

Figure 11
Join strips as shown to
make a long strip.

Step 5. Join the block rows with the pieced strips as shown in Figure 12; press seams toward strips.

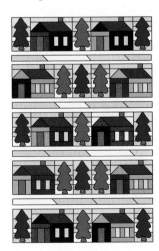

Figure 12
Join the block rows
with the pieced strips.

Step 6. Cut two strips each 1 1/2" x 32 1/2" and 1 1/2" x 40 1/2" green tone-on-tone. Sew the longer strips to opposite sides and shorter strips to the top and bottom; press seams toward strips.

Step 7. Cut four 1 1/2" x 22" strips from each house fat quarter. Join one strip of each fabric with right sides together along length to make a strip set; repeat for four strip sets in the same color order. Press seams in one direction.

Step 8. Subcut strip sets into 3 1/2" segments.

Step 9. Join six segments to make a side strip; remove six strips from one end as shown in Figure 13. Repeat for two side strips; press seams in one direction. Sew a side strip to two opposite sides of the pieced center; press seams away from pieced strips.

Figure 13
Join 6 segments to make a side
strip; remove 6 strips from 1 end.

Step 10. Cut four 3 1/2" x 3 1/2" squares brown check for O.

Step 11. Join four segments to make a top strip. Repeat for bottom strip; press seams in one direction.

Step 12. Sew an O square to opposite ends of each pieced strip as shown in Figure 14. Sew the strips to the top and bottom of the pieced center; press seams away from pieced strips.

Figure 14
Sew an O square to opposite
ends of each pieced strip.

Step 13. Cut and piece two strips each 1 1/2" x 40 1/2" and 1 1/2" x 48 1/2" green tone-on tone. Sew the longer strips to opposite sides and shorter strips to the top and bottom of the pieced center; press seams toward strips.

Step 14. Prepare for quilting and quilt as desired referring to the General Instructions. ***Note:*** *The project shown was machine-quilted in a meandering pattern in the cream/off-white pieces and in the ditch of border strips using cream machine-quilting thread.*

Step 15. Prepare 5 1/2 yards green tone-on-tone binding and apply referring to the General Instructions to finish. ❖

Pattern continued on page 109

Dragonfly Meadow

By Connie Rand

This is one of those quilts that looks much more complicated than it really is.
Use your favorite fat quarters to make your own version.

Project Specifications

Skill Level: Beginner

Quilt Size: 45" x 45"

Block Size: 10" x 10"

Number of Blocks: 16

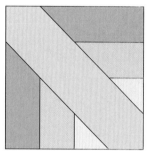

Classic A
10" x 10" Block

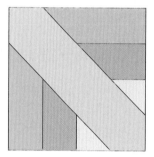

Classic B
10" x 10" Block

Materials

- 1 fat quarter each yellow and blue small dragonfly prints
- 1 fat quarter each yellow and blue small floral prints
- 2 fat quarters each pink small dragonfly print and pink small floral print
- 1 fat quarter blue bunny print
- 4 fat quarters pink large dragonfly print (1 yard)
- Backing 49" x 49"
- Batting 49" x 49"
- 5 1/2 yards self-made or purchased binding
- Neutral color all-purpose thread
- Cream machine-quilting thread
- Basic sewing supplies and tools

Instructions

Step 1. Prepare templates for pieces B, C and D using pattern pieces given; cut as directed on each piece.

Step 2. Cut three 3 3/8" x 22" strips yellow small floral print; subcut each strip into 3 3/8" square segments. Cut each square in half on one diagonal to make A triangles; you will need 32 A triangles.

Dragonfly Meadow
Placement Diagram
45" x 45"

Step 3. Sew A to B to C, and AR to BR to C as shown in Figure 1 and referring to Color Key for fabric placement in each unit.

Step 4. Join A-B-C and AR-BR-C with D as shown in Figure 2 to make one each A and B blocks; repeat for eight of each block.

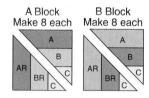

Figure 1
Sew A to B to C and AR to BR to C in color combinations shown.

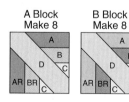

Figure 2
Join A-B-C and AR-BR-C units with D as shown.

Step 5. Join two A blocks with two B blocks to make an X row referring to Figure 3. Repeat with two blocks each to make a Y row, again referring to Figure 3. Press seams in one direction.

Step 6. Join rows referring to the Placement Diagram; press seams in one direction.

Step 7. Cut four 3" x 10 1/2" rectangles each yellow small floral print, blue and yellow small dragonfly prints, and pink large dragonfly print for E.

Step 8. Cut four 3" x 3" squares blue bunny print for F.

Step 9. Join one E rectangle of each fabric on short ends to make an E border strip as shown in Figure 4; repeat for four E border strips. Press seams in one direction.

X Row
Make 2

Y Row
Make 2

Figure 3
Join blocks to make X and Y rows.

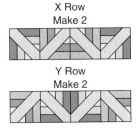

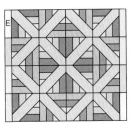

Figure 5
Sew an E strip to opposite sides of the pieced center.

Figure 6
Sew F to each end of remaining E strips and sew to top and bottom.

| E | | | |

Figure 4
Sew 4 E pieces to make a border strip.

Step 10. Sew an E border strip to opposite sides of the pieced center as shown in Figure 5; press seams toward strips.

Step 11. Sew an F square to each end of the remaining E border strips; press seams toward F. Sew the E-F strips to pieced center to complete quilt top as shown in Figure 6.

Step 12. Prepare for quilting and quilt as desired referring to the General Instructions. *Note: The quilt shown was machine-quilted in the ditch of seams and in double parallel lines in the D pieces using cream machine-quilting thread.*

Step 13. Apply self-made or purchased binding referring to the General Instructions to finish. ❖

COLOR KEY
☐ Pink large dragonfly print
☐ Pink small dragonfly print
☐ Yellow small dragonfly print
☐ Blue small dragonfly print
■ Pink small floral print
☐ Yellow small floral print
■ Blue small floral print
☐ Blue bunny print

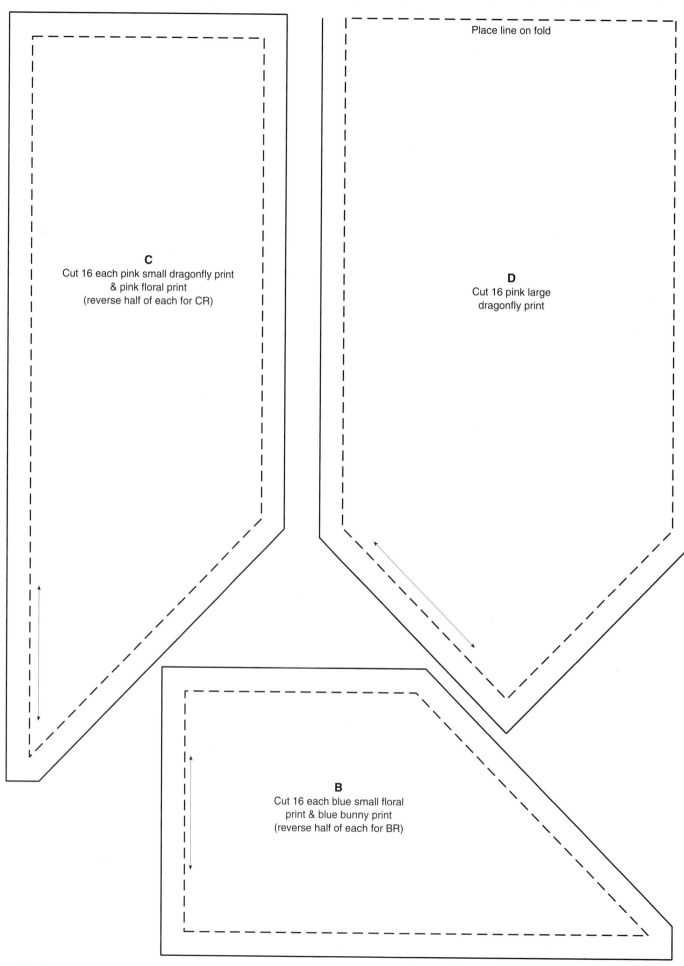

Place line on fold

C
Cut 16 each pink small dragonfly print
& pink floral print
(reverse half of each for CR)

D
Cut 16 pink large
dragonfly print

B
Cut 16 each blue small floral
print & blue bunny print
(reverse half of each for BR)

Hearts United

By Pearl Louise Krush

*Pieced hearts using patriotic prints share the united spirit
of the people of the United States during trying times.*

Project Specifications

Skill Level: Beginner

Quilt Size: 83" x 83"

Block Size: 9" x 9"

Number of Blocks: 36

Nine-Patch
9" x 9" Block

Heart
9" x 9" Block

Materials

- 1 fat quarter dark blue print
- 2 fat quarters cream tone-on-tones
- 6 fat quarters white-with-red-and-blue prints (WRB)
- 8 fat quarters red-white-and-blue prints (RWB)
- 5/8 yard red tone-on-tone
- 1 1/2 yards stripe star print
- 2 5/8 yards blue tone-on-tone
- Backing 87" x 87"
- Batting 87" x 87"
- All-purpose thread to match fabrics
- White machine-quilting thread
- Basic sewing tools and supplies, rotary cutter, mat and ruler

Instructions

Note: All fat quarter fabric width is considered to be 22".

Making Heart Blocks

Step 1. Cut three 5" by fabric width strips dark blue print; subcut strips into 4 1/2" segments for A. You will need 12 A pieces.

Step 2. Cut six 2 1/2" by fabric width strips cream tone-on-tones; subcut strips into 2 1/2" square segments for B. You will need 48 B squares.

Step 3. Mark a diagonal line from corner to corner on the wrong side of each B square.

Step 4. Referring to Figure 1, place a B square on one corner of A; stitch on the marked line and trim seam to 1/4". Press B to the right side. Place a second B square on the opposite corner of A, stitch, trim and press to complete one A-B unit. Repeat for 12 A-B units.

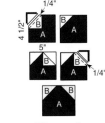

Figure 1
Make an A-B
unit as shown.

Step 5. Cut 24 strips 1 1/2" by fabric width RWB and 18 strips WRB prints 1 1/2" by fabric width.

Step 6. Join two RWB strips with two WRB strips with right sides together along length to make a strip set as shown in Figure 2; press seams toward darker fabric strips. Repeat for three strip sets.

Figure 2
Join fabric strips; subcut
into 5" segments for C.

Step 7. Subcut strip sets into twelve 5" segments for C, again referring to Figure 2.

Step 8. Complete B-C units as in Step 4 for A-B units and referring to Figure 3.

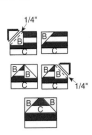

Figure 3
Make a B-C
unit as shown.

Step 9. Join two of the remaining WRB strips with three of the remaining RWB strips with right sides together along length to make a strip set as shown in Figure 4. Repeat for six strip sets.

Step 10. Subcut strip sets into twelve 9 1/2" segments for E, again referring to Figure 4.

Figure 4
Join fabric strips; subcut into
9 1/2" segments for E.

Step 11. Cut three 5" by fabric width strips cream tone-on-tones; subcut strips into ten 5" segments for D. Mark a line from corner to corner on the wrong side of each D square.

Step 12. Complete D-E units as in Step 4 and referring to Figure 5; repeat for 12 D-E units.

Step 13. Join one A-B, one B-C and one D-E to complete one Heart block as shown in Figure 6; repeat for 12 Heart blocks.

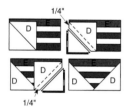

Figure 5
Make D-E units as shown.

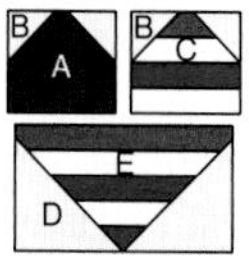

Figure 6
Join 1 A-B, 1 B-C unit
and 1 D-E to complete
1 Heart block.

Making Nine-Patch Blocks

Step 1. Cut six 5 1/2" by fabric width strips WRB for G. Cut twelve 2 1/2" by fabric width strips RWB for F.

Step 2. Sew two RWB strips to one WRB strip with right sides together along length; press seams toward darker fabric. Repeat for six strip sets.

Step 3. Subcut strip sets into 2 1/2" segments as shown in Figure 7 to make F-G units. You will need 48 F-G units.

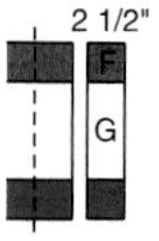

Figure 7
Subcut strip sets int
2 1/2" segments to
make F-G units.

Step 4. Cut six 5 1/2" by fabric width strips RWB for H and twelve 2 1/2" by fabric width strips WRB for G.

Step 5. Sew two G strips to an H strip with right sides together along length; press seams toward darker fabric. Repeat for six strip sets.

Step 6. Subcut strip sets into 5 1/2" segments to make G-H units as shown in Figure 8; you will need 24 G-H units.

Step 7. Join two F-G units with one G-H unit to complete one Nine-Patch block as shown in Figure 9; press seams away from the G-H units.

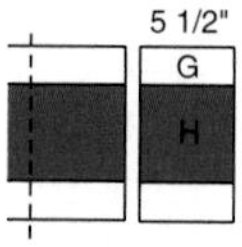

Figure 8
Subcut strip sets into 5 1/2"
segments to make G-H units.

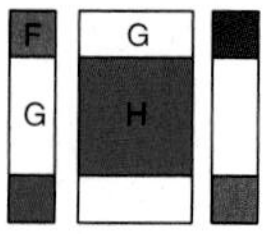

Figure 9
Join 2 F-G units with 1 G-H unit
to complete 1 Nine-Patch block.

Completing the Quilt

Step 1. Cut six 9 1/2" by fabric width strips blue tone-on-tone (these are 42" long). Subcut strips into 2 1/2" segments to make J sashing strips; you will need 84 J pieces.

Step 2. Cut four 2 1/2" by fabric width strips red tone-on-tone; subcut strips into 2 1/2" square segments for K. You will need 49 K squares.

Step 3. Join seven K squares and six J pieces to make a sashing row as shown in Figure 10; repeat for seven sashing rows. Press seams toward K.

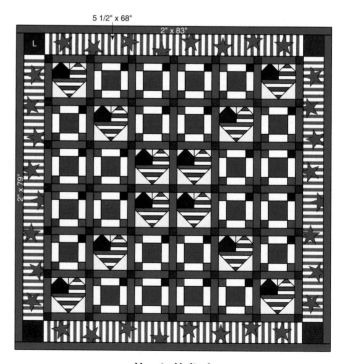

Hearts United
Placement Diagram
83" x 83"

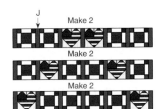

Figure 10
Join 7 K squares and 6 J pieces
to make a sashing row.

Step 4. Join two Heart blocks with four Nine-Patch blocks and seven J pieces to make block rows as shown in Figure 11; repeat for two rows each. Press seams toward J.

Step 5. Join the block rows with the sashing rows referring to the Placement Diagram for positioning of the rows; press seams toward sashing rows.

Make 2

Make 2

Make 2

Figure 11
Join 2 Heart blocks with 4
Nine-Patch blocks and 7 J
pieces to make block rows.

Step 6. Cut and piece four strips each stripe star print 6" x 68 1/2" for M. Cut four 6" x 6" squares red tone-on-tone for L.

Step 7. Sew an M strip to opposite sides of the pieced center; press seams toward M.

Step 8. Sew an L square to each end of M; press seams toward L. Sew an L-M strip to the top and bottom of the pieced center; press seams toward L-M strips.

Step 9. Cut and piece two strips each 2 1/2" x 79 1/2" and 2 1/2" x 83 1/2" blue tone-on-tone; sew the shorter strips to opposite sides and longer strips to the top and bottom of the pieced center; press seams toward strips.

Step 10. Prepare for quilting and quilt as desired referring to the General Instructions. ***Note:*** *The project shown was machine-quilted in an allover design using white machine-quilting thread.*

Step 11. Cut nine strips 2 1/4" by fabric width blue tone-on-tone. Prepare and apply self-made binding referring to the General Instructions to finish. ❖

Stars & Stripes Table Quilt

By Kate Laucomer

Stars and stripes combine to make a patriotic table quilt.

Project Note

If you want to save time, substitute a red-and-white stripe for the pieced stripe sections. You may not be able to find two different size stripes, but no matter what the size, it will work.

Project Specifications

Skill Level: Beginner

Project Size: 24" x 24"

Block Size: 3" x 3" and 6" x 6"

Number of Blocks: 4 small and 5 large

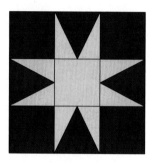

Star
3" x 3" Block
6" x 6" Block

Materials

- 1 fat quarter yellow tone-on-tone
- 2 fat quarters white-on-white print
- 2 fat quarters red tone-on-tone
- 2 fat quarters navy star print
- Backing 28" x 28"
- Batting 28" x 28"
- Red, white and navy all-purpose thread
- Black marker
- Basic sewing supplies and tools, rotary cutter, mat and ruler

Instructions

Piecing Star Blocks

Step 1. Cut four 1 1/2" x 1 1/2" squares (A) and five 2 1/2" squares (B) yellow tone-on-tone.

Step 2. Cut 32 squares 1 1/2" x 1 1/2" (C) and 40 squares 2 1/2" x 2 1/2" (D) navy star print.

Step 3. Copy 16 small and 20 large star point foundations. Trace over lines with a black marker.

Step 4. To piece one small star point, place a C square on the marked side of the paper; trim to make 1/4" larger than the space 1 piece as shown in Figure 1. Pin to the unmarked side of the paper over space 1.

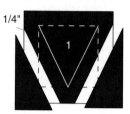

Figure 1
Place a C square on the
marked side of the paper;
trim to make 1/4" larger
than space 1.

Step 5. Cut yellow tone-on-tone pieces to fit over spaces 2 and 3, adding seam allowance all around.

Step 6. Pin piece 2 right sides together on piece 1 and fold back to be sure that piece 2 will cover the entire area of space 2 plus seam allowance. Fold back, turn paper over and stitch as shown in Figure 2; press piece 2 to the right side. Repeat with piece 3. *Note: Set the machine stitch length to a very small stitch to make removing paper easier.*

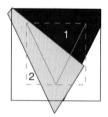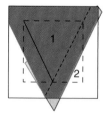

Figure 2
Pin piece 2 right sides together with piece 1.
Turn paper over; stitch on marked line.

Step 7. Trim excess fabric even with the paper foundation; repeat for 16 small star points. Remove paper backing.

Step 8. Repeat with large star point foundations and D squares for piece 1 to make 20 large star points. Remove paper backing.

Step 9. Sew a small star point between two C squares to make a C row as shown in Figure 3; repeat for eight rows. Join a large star point between two D squares to make a D row, again referring to Figure 3; repeat for 10 D rows.

Figure 3
Sew a small star point between 2 C squares to make a C row; repeat with D squares and large star point to make a D row.

Step 10. Join two small star points with one A square to make an A row as shown in Figure 4; repeat for four A rows. Join two large star points with one B square to make a B row, again referring to Figure 4; repeat for five B rows. Press seams toward darker fabric.

Figure 4
Join 2 small star points with 1 A square to make an A row; repeat with B square and large star points to make a B row.

Step 11. Join two C rows with one A row to complete one small Star block as shown in Figure 5; press seams toward darker fabric. Repeat for four small Star blocks.

Figure 5
Join 2 C rows with 1 A row to make a small Star block.

Step 12. Repeat Step 11 with two D rows and one B row to complete one large Star block, referring to Figure 6; repeat for five large Star blocks. Press seams toward darker fabric.

Figure 6
Join 2 D rows and 1 B row to complete 1 large Star block.

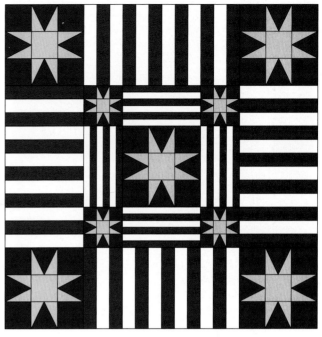

Stars & Stripes Table Quilt
Placement Diagram
24" x 24"

Center Section

Step 1. Cut six 1" x 22" strips each red tone-on-tone and white-on-white print.

Step 2. Sew a red strip to a white strip with right sides together along length; press seams toward darker fabric. Repeat for six strip sets. Join three strip sets with right sides together along length as shown in Figure 7; press seams toward darker fabric. Repeat for a second strip set.

Step 3. Cut four 6 1/2" segments from the strip sets for E as shown in Figure 8.

Figure 7
Join 3 strip sets with right
sides together along length.

6 1/2"

E

Figure 8
Subcut strip sets into
6 1/2" E segments.

E

Figure 9
Sew E to opposite sides
of a large Star block.

E

Figure 10
Sew a small Star block to
opposite ends of E.

Step 4. Sew E to opposites sides of a large Star block as shown in Figure 9; press seams toward E.

Step 5. Sew a small Star block to opposite ends of E as shown in Figure 10; press seams toward E. Repeat for two rows.

Step 6. Sew a small Star strip to opposite sides of the large Star strip to complete the pieced center section as shown in Figure 11; press seams away from center.

Figure 11
Sew a small Star strip to opposite
sides of the large Star strip to
complete the pieced center section.

Outside Stars & Stripes Border

Step 1. Cut 12 strips each 1 1/2" x 22" red
tone-on-tone and white-on-white print.

Step 2. Sew a red strip to a white strip with right sides
together along length; repeat for 12 strip sets. Press
seams toward red strips.

Step 3. Join six strip sets with right sides together
along length; press seams toward darker fabric. Repeat
for a second strip set.

Step 4. Subcut strip sets into four 6 1/2" segments for
F as shown in Figure 12.

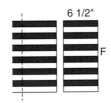

Figure 12
Subcut strip sets into four
6 1/2" segments for F.

Step 5. Sew F to opposite sides of the pieced center
section as shown in Figure 13; press seams away from
center section.

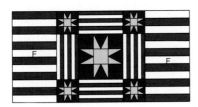

Figure 13
Sew F to opposite sides of
the pieced center section.

Step 6. Sew a large Star block to each end of the
remaining F pieces as shown in Figure 14; press seams
away from blocks. Repeat for two strips.

Step 7. Join the pieced sections to complete the pieced
top as shown in Figure 15.

Figure 14
Sew a large Star block to each
end of the remaining F pieces.

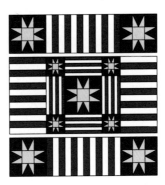

Figure 15
Join the pieced sections to
complete the pieced top.

Finishing

Step 1. Prepare for quilting and quilt as desired referring to the General Instructions. *Note: The quilt shown
was machine-quilted in a curving line in the stripe
pieces and in the
ditch of seams in the
pieced blocks using
all-purpose thread to
match fabrics.*

Step 2. Prepare 3 1/8
yards of navy star
print binding and
apply referring to the
General Instructions
to finish. ❖

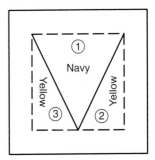

Small Star Point Foundation
Make 16 copies

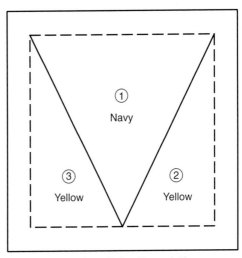

Large Star Point Foundation
Make 20 copies

United We Stand

By Julie Weaver

A pieced flag design expresses our feelings for the red, white and blue.

Project Specifications

Skill Level: Beginner

Quilt Size: 20" x 44"

Block Size: 6" x 6"

Number of Blocks: 6

Materials

- ◆ 1 fat quarter light blue tone-on-tone
- ◆ 1 fat quarter dark blue tone-on-tone
- ◆ 2 fat quarters cream tone-on-tones
- ◆ 2 fat quarters white tone-on-tones
- ◆ 4 fat quarters red tone-on-tones
- ◆ Backing 24" x 48"
- ◆ Batting 24" x 48"
- ◆ 3 3/4 yards self-made or purchased red binding
- ◆ All-purpose thread to match fabrics
- ◆ Red, cream and blue machine-quilting thread
- ◆ Basic sewing tools and supplies, rotary cutter, mat and ruler

Instructions

Making Star Blocks

Note: Fabric width is considered 22".

Step 1. Cut one 2 7/8" by fabric width strip from each cream/white tone-on-tone; subcut each strip into three 2 7/8" square segments. You will need a total of 12 squares. From the same strips, cut a total of six 2 1/2" x 2 1/2" squares for C.

Step 2. Cut four 2 7/8" by fabric width strips light blue tone-on-tone; subcut into 2 7/8" square segments. You will need 24 squares.

Step 3. Cut two 2 7/8" by fabric width dark blue tone-on-tone; subcut into 2 7/8" square segments. You will need 12 squares.

Step 4. Layer one 2 7/8" x 2 7/8" square each light blue tone-on-tone with a cream/white tone-on-tone square with right sides together. Draw a line from corner to corner on the lighter square. Sew 1/4" on each side of the marked line as shown in Figure 1.

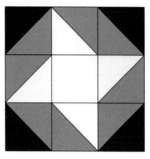

Star
6" x 6" Block

Step 5. Cut on the drawn line; press seam to the darker fabric side to make A units as shown in Figure 2. Repeat for 24 A units.

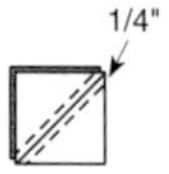

Figure 1
Sew 1/4" on each side of the marked line.

Figure 2
Cut on the drawn line; press seam to the darker fabric side to make A units.

Step 6. Repeat Steps 4 and 5 with 2 7/8" x 2 7/8" dark blue tone-on-tone and light blue tone-on-tone squares to make 24 B units as shown in Figure 3.

Step 7. Join four each A and B units with one C square to complete one Star block referring to Figure 4; repeat for six blocks.

Figure 3
Make B units as shown.

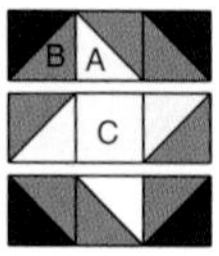

Figure 4
Join 4 each A and B units with 1 C square to complete 1 Star block.

Making Flying Geese Units

Step 1. Cut six 2 1/2" by fabric width strips from each red tone-on-tone; subcut three strips each fabric into 4 1/2" segments for D and the remaining strips into 2 1/2" squares for E. You will need 45 D segments and 90 E squares. Draw a line from corner to corner on the wrong side of each E square.

Step 2. Mixing fabrics, place an E square on D as shown in Figure 5; sew on marked line. Trim seam to 1/4" and press E to the right side as shown in Figure 6. Repeat on the opposite end to make a Flying Geese unit as shown in Figure 7; repeat for 45 red Flying Geese units.

Figure 5
Place an E square on D.

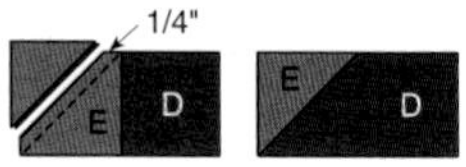

Figure 6
Trim seam to 1/4" and press E to the right side.

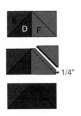

Figure 7
Complete a red Flying
Geese unit as shown.

Step 3. Cut four 2 1/2" by fabric width strips from one cream/white tone-on-tone; subcut two strips into 4 1/2" segments for D. Subcut the remaining two strips into 2 1/2" segments for E. Repeat with each of the remaining fabrics to make a total of 30 D pieces and 60 E squares. Draw a line from corner to corner on the wrong side of each E square.

Step 4. Make 30 cream/white Flying Geese units as in Step 2 and referring to Figure 8.

Figure 8
Complete a cream/white
Flying Geese unit as shown.

Quilt Top Assembly

Step 1. Join three Star blocks to make a row as shown in Figure 9; repeat for two rows. Press seams in one direction.

Figure 9
Join 3 Star blocks to make a row.

Step 2. Cut four 1 1/2" by fabric width strips dark blue tone-on-tone and two 1 1/2" by fabric width strips light blue tone-on-tone.

Step 3. Cut two segments each 2 1/2", 3 1/2" and 5 1/2" from dark blue tone-on-tone strips and four 3 1/2" segments from the light blue tone-on-tone strips. Set aside remaining strips for top and bottom borders.

Step 4. To make one border strip, begin with a dark blue 2 1/2" segment. With right sides together, lay a light blue 3 1/2" segment perpendicular to the dark blue segment with top and side edges even as shown in Figure 10. Draw a diagonal line from left to right and sew on the line as shown in Figure 11. Trim and press. Repeat with a 5 1/2" dark blue segment.

Figure 10
With right sides together,
lay a light blue 3 1/2"
segment perpendicular to
the dark blue strip with top
and side edges even.

Figure 11
Draw a diagonal line
from left to right and
sew on the line.

Step 5. Join the pieced segments as in Step 4 and referring to Figure 12. Add a 3 1/2" dark blue segment to the light blue end to complete one border strip as shown in Figure 13; repeat for two border strips.

Figure 12
Join the 2
pieced segments.

Figure 13
Add a 3 1/2" dark blue segment
to complete 1 border strip.

Step 6. Carefully pin the pieced strips to the sides of the star section, making sure that, when sewn with a 1/4" seam, the lights and darks meet to make a continuous diagonal flow.

Step 7. Cut remaining dark blue tone-on-tone strips into two 3 1/2", two 4 1/2" and four 5 1/2" segments. Cut light blue tone-on-tone strips into six 3 1/2" segments.

United We Stand
Placement Diagram
20" x 44"

Step 8. Referring to Steps 4 and 5 and Figure 14, join dark and light blue segments to complete top and bottom border strips. Carefully pin strips to the top and bottom of the star section as in Step 6.

Figure 14
Join segments to make top and
bottom border strips as shown.

Step 9. Join 15 red Flying Geese units to make a strip as shown in Figure 15; press seams in one direction. Repeat for three red strips.

Figure 15
Join 15 red Flying Geese
units to make a strip.

Step 10. Join 15 cream/white Flying Geese units to make a strip as shown in Figure 16; press seams in one direction. Repeat for two cream/white strips.

Figure 16
Join 15 cream/white Flying
Geese units to make a strip.

Step 11. Join the Flying Geese strips as shown in Figure 17; press seams in one direction.

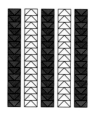

Figure 17
Join the Flying
Geese strips.

Step 12. Sew the Flying Geese strip section to the star section to complete the pieced top; press seams toward star section.

Step 13. Prepare for quilting and quilt as desired referring to the General Instructions. ***Note:*** *The project shown was machine-quilted in the ditch of seams with machine-quilting thread to match fabrics.*

Step 14. Apply self-made or purchased red binding referring to the General Instructions to finish. ❖

Maple Leaf Ragtime

By Willow Sirch

The autumn colors of maple leaves were the inspiration for this gorgeous classic scrap quilt.

Project Notes

Fat quarters of Bali prints and other hand-printed cottons, along with a few small calico prints, were used to make the sample quilt. We recommend washing and ironing all fabrics before using in the quilt. Pay special attention to hand-dyed reds as these may require more than one washing to make colorfast.

Project Specifications

Skill Level: Beginner

Quilt Size: 48" x 48"

Block Size: 8" x 8"

Number of Blocks: 20

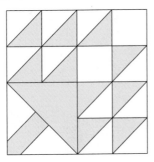

Maple Leaf
8" x 8" Block

Materials

- 20 different fat quarters in brick red, gold, orange and olive green tones
- 1/2 yard beige mottled for binding
- 1 1/4 yards muslin
- Backing 52" x 52"
- Batting 52" x 52"
- All-purpose thread to match fabrics
- White hand-quilting thread
- Basic sewing tools and supplies, rotary cutter, mat and ruler

Instructions

Step 1. Cut one 2 7/8" x 22" strip from each fat quarter; subcut into 2 7/8" square segments. Cut each square in half on one diagonal to make A triangles; you will need 10 dark A triangles for each block.

Step 2. Cut one 4 7/8" x 4 7/8" square from each fat quarter; cut in half on one diagonal to make B triangles. Set aside one triangle of each fabric for another project.

Step 3. Prepare template for E using pattern given; cut one E piece from each fat quarter.

Step 4. Cut three 2 1/2" by fabric width strips muslin; subcut strips into 2 1/2" square segments for C. You will need two C squares for each block and a total of 40 for the whole quilt.

Step 5. Cut eight 2 7/8" by fabric width strips muslin; subcut strips into 2 7/8" square segments. You will need 100 squares. Cut each square in half on one diagonal to make muslin A triangles; you will need 10 muslin A triangles for each block and a total of 200 for the whole quilt.

Step 6. Cut two 4 3/8" by fabric width strips muslin; subcut strips into 4 3/8" square segments. You will need 10 squares. Cut each square on both diagonals to make D triangles as shown in Figure 1; you will need 40 D triangles.

Step 7. To piece one block, sew a muslin A to a colored A to make a triangle/square unit as shown in Figure 2; repeat for 10 same-fabric A units. Press seams toward darker fabric.

Figure 1
Cut the 4 7/8"
squares on both
diagonals to make
D triangles.

Figure 2
Sew a muslin A to a
colored A to make a
triangle/square unit.

Step 8. Sew a muslin D to opposite sides of a same-fabric E as shown in Figure 3; press seams toward E.

Step 9. Sew the E-D unit to B as shown in Figure 4; press seam toward B.

Figure 3
Sew a muslin D to
opposite sides of a
same-fabric E.

Figure 4
Sew the E-D
unit to B.

Step 10. Join the pieced units as shown in Figure 5 to make rows; join the rows to complete one Maple Leaf block. Press seams in one direction. Repeat for 20 blocks.

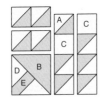

Figure 5
Join the pieced units as shown
to make rows; join the rows to
complete 1 Maple Leaf block.

Figure 8
Join 3 blocks to
make a strip; repeat
for a reverse strip.

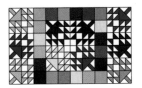

Figure 9
Sew the block strips
to opposite sides of
the pieced center.

Step 16. Join five blocks to make a strip as shown in Figure 10; repeat for a reverse strip, again referring to Figure 10. Sew the block strips to the top and bottom of the pieced center referring to Figure 11; press seams toward F strips.

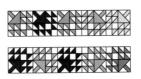

Figure 10
Join 5 blocks to make a strip;
repeat for a reverse strip.

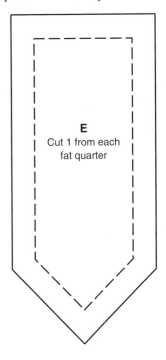

Figure 11
Sew the block strips to
the top and bottom of
the pieced center.

Maple Leaf Ragtime
Placement Diagram
48" x 48"

Step 11. Join four blocks to make the pieced center referring to Figure 6; press seams in one direction.

Step 12. Cut one strip 4 1/2" x 22" from each fat quarter; subcut strips into 4 1/2" square segments for F. You will need 64 F squares; set aside remaining squares for another project.

Step 13. Join four different F squares to make a strip; press seams in one direction. Repeat for two strips. Sew a strip to opposite sides of the pieced center as shown in Figure 7; press seams toward pieced strips.

Figure 6
Join 4 blocks to make
the pieced center.

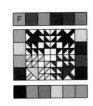

Figure 7
Sew a strip to opposite
sides, and top and bottom
of the pieced center.

Step 14. Join six different F squares to make a strip; press seams in one direction. Repeat for two strips. Sew a strip to the top and bottom of the pieced center, again referring to Figure 7; press seams toward pieced strips.

Step 15. Join three blocks to make a strip as shown in Figure 8; repeat for a reverse strip, again referring to Figure 8. Sew the block strips to opposite sides of the pieced center referring to Figure 9; press seams toward F strips.

Step 17. Join 10 F squares to make a strip; repeat for two strips. Sew to opposite sides of the pieced center; press seams toward F strips. Join 12 F squares to make a strip; repeat for two strips. Sew to the top and bottom of the pieced center to complete the pieced top; press seams toward F strips.

Step 18. Prepare for quilting and quilt as desired referring to the General Instructions. *Note: The project shown was hand-quilted 1/4" from seams in the muslin pieces using white hand quilting thread.*

Step 19. Prepare 6 yards beige mottled binding and apply referring to the General Instructions to finish. ❖

E
Cut 1 from each
fat quarter

Pretty Maids

By Sue Harvey

Turn flower-color fat quarters into a lap quilt of "pretty maids all in a row."

Project Specifications

Skill Level: Beginner

Quilt Size: 56" x 68"

Block Size: 10" x 12"

Number of Blocks: 9

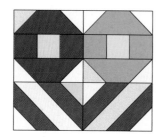

Pretty Maids
10" x 12" Block

Materials

- 1 yellow print fat quarter
- 4 green print fat quarters
- 6 flower-color print fat quarters
- 8 cream print fat quarters
- 1 1/2 yards floral print
- Backing 60" x 72"
- Batting 60" x 72"
- All-purpose thread to match fabrics
- Basic sewing tools and supplies, rotary cutter, mat and ruler

Instructions

Note: Fabrics are referred to as yellow, green, cream and flower throughout these instructions. All strips for this project are cut along the 22" length of the fat quarters.

Step 1. Cut 26 strips 2 1/2" x 22" from four cream fat quarters; subcut each strip into 2 1/2" squares for A. You will need 204 A squares. Mark a diagonal line on the wrong side of each square.

Step 2. From remaining cream fat quarters, cut the following: three strips 4 7/8" x 22"—subcut into twelve 4 7/8" squares for D; four strips 4 1/2" x 22" for E; and six strips 4 1/2" x 22"—subcut into four 2 1/2" segments for F, eight 6 1/2" segments for G, two 8 1/2" segments for H and four 4 1/2" squares for J.

Step 3. Cut two strips 4 7/8" x 22" from each green fat quarter; subcut each strip into 4 7/8" square segments for D. You will need 30 green D squares.

Step 4. Place an A square on opposite corners of each green D square as shown in Figure 1. Stitch on the marked diagonal line, trim seam allowance to 1/4" and press A open as shown in Figure 2. Cut the D square on the unstitched diagonal to make two A-D units as shown in Figure 3; repeat for 60 A-D units.

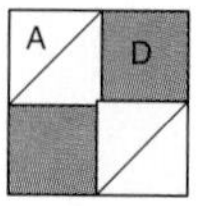

Figure 1
Place an A square on opposite corners of a green D.

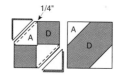

Figure 2
Stitch on the diagonal line, trim seam allowance and press A open.

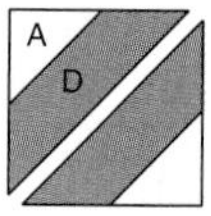

Figure 3
Cut the D square on the unstitched diagonal to make 2 A-D units.

Step 5. Place two cream E strips wrong sides together. Cut one end of the layered strips with a 45-degree angle as shown in Figure 4; subcut layered strips into 1 7/8" segments to make E and ER segments, again referring to Figure 4. Repeat with remaining E strips to make nine each E and ER segments.

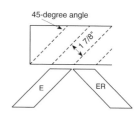

Figure 4
Cut E and ER segments from the layered strips as shown.

Step 6. Cut six strips 2 1/2" x 22" from one flower fat quarter; subcut into 12 segments 2 1/2" x 6 1/2" for B and 12 squares 2 1/2" x 2 1/2" for C. Repeat with each flower fat quarter.

Step 7. Cut five yellow strips 2 1/2" x 22"; subcut into 36 squares 2 1/2" x 2 1/2" for C.

Step 8. To piece one flower unit, choose two B segments and two C squares of one flower color. Place an A square on each end of B as shown in Figure 5; stitch on the marked diagonal line, trim seam allowance to 1/4" and press A open. Repeat for two A-B units.

Step 9. Sew a yellow C between the two flower C squares.

Step 10. Sew the C strip between the A-B units to complete one flower unit as shown in Figure 6; repeat Steps 8–10 to make 36 flower units.

Figure 5
Place A on each end of
B; stitch, trim and press
to make an A-B unit.

Figure 6
Complete 1 flower
unit as shown.

Step 11. To piece one stem unit, sew an A-D unit to opposite sides of E as shown in Figure 7; repeat with ER.

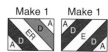

Make 1   Make 1

Figure 7
Sew an A-D unit to
opposite sides of E.

Step 12. Join the pieced units to complete one stem unit as shown in Figure 8; repeat for nine stem units.

Figure 8
Complete 1 stem
unit as shown.

Step 13. Join two flower units with one stem unit to complete one Pretty Maids block as shown in Figure 9; repeat for nine blocks.

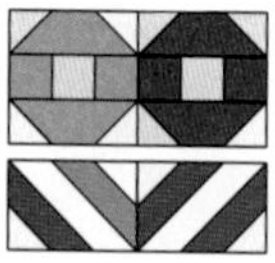

Figure 9
Join 2 flower units
with 1 stem unit to
complete 1 block.

Step 14. Join three blocks to make a row; repeat for three block rows.

Step 15. Join six flower units to make a sashing row; repeat for three sashing rows.

Step 16. Join the block rows with the sashing rows as shown in Figure 10.

Figure 10
Join the block rows
with the sashing rows.

Step 17. Cut each cream D square on one diagonal to make triangles. Sew an A-D unit to each triangle to complete one leaf unit as shown in Figure 11; repeat for 24 leaf units.

Figure 11
Complete 1 leaf
unit as shown.

Step 18. Join six leaf units with two F, two G and one H segment to make a side strip as shown in Figure 12; repeat. Sew a strip to each side of the pieced center referring to the Placement Diagram for positioning of strips.

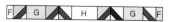

Figure 12
Join 6 leaf units with F, G and H
segments to make a side strip.

Step 19. Join six leaf units with two G segments and two J squares to make an end strip as shown in Figure 13; repeat. Sew a strip to each end of the pieced center referring to the Placement Diagram for positioning of strips.

Step 20. Cut four strips 1 1/2" x 22" from each green fat quarter; cut each strip in half to make 11" lengths. Join strips randomly on short ends to make a long strip; press seams in one direction. Cut into two strips each 46 1/2" long and 56 1/2" long.

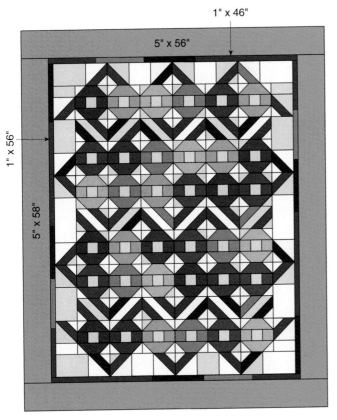

Pretty Maids
Placement Diagram
56" x 68"

Labels on diagram: 1" x 46", 5" x 56", 1" x 56", 5" x 58"

Figure 13
Join 6 leaf units with G segments
and J squares to make an end strip.

Step 21. Sew the longer strips to opposite long sides of the pieced center and the shorter strips to the ends; press seams toward strips.

Step 22. Cut and piece two strips each 5 1/2" x 56 1/2" and 5 1/2" x 58 1/2" floral print. Sew the longer strips to opposite long sides of the pieced center and the shorter strips to the ends; press seams toward strips.

Step 23. Sandwich batting between the completed top and prepared backing piece; pin or baste to hold.

Step 24. Hand- or machine-quilt as desired. *Note: The sample shown was professionally machine-quilted in an allover pattern. Trim backing and batting even with the quilted top.*

Step 25. Cut seven strips floral print 2 1/4" by fabric width. Prepare and apply self-made binding referring to the General Instructions to finish. ❖

Evergreen Lane
Continued from page 89

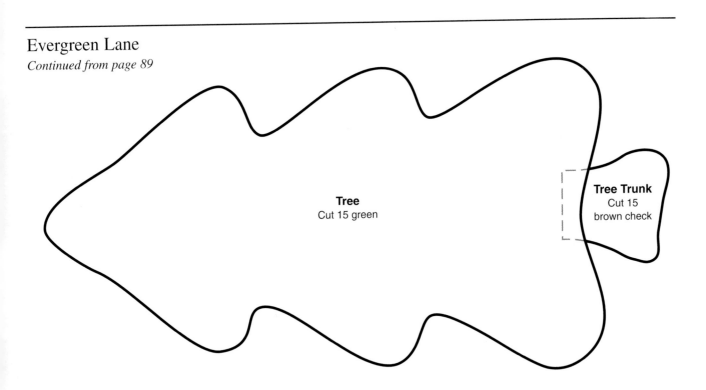

Tree
Cut 15 green

Tree Trunk
Cut 15
brown check

3-D Quilting

Folding, gathering, ruching and fraying combine to create flowers and grapes, to make your fat-quarter quilts and projects come alive with depth and beauty.

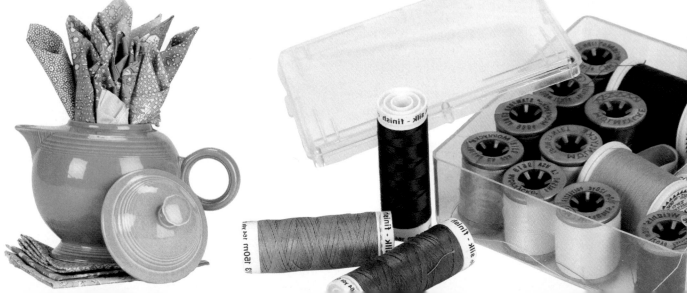

Ruched Roses & Baskets

By Pearl Louise Krush

Appliquéd leaves and ruched roses fill the pieced baskets on this pretty wall quilt.

Project Specifications

Skill Level: Intermediate

Quilt Size: 35 3/4" x 35 3/4"

Blocks Size: 9" x 9"

Number of Blocks: 5

Materials

- 1 fat quarter dark green check
- 1 fat quarter gold check
- 1 fat quarter light green mottled
- 1 fat quarter each light and medium rose tone-on-tones
- 1/3 yard green tone-on-tone
- 1/2 yard dark rose tone-on-tone
- 1/2 yard dark green floral
- 1 yard cream tone-on-tone
- Backing 40" x 40"
- Batting 40" x 40"
- All-purpose thread to match fabrics
- Cream machine-quilting thread
- Basic sewing tools and supplies, rotary cutter, mat and ruler

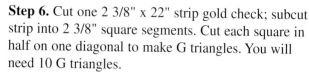

Rose Basket
9" x 9" Block

Instructions

Basket Blocks

Step 1. Cut two 2" by fabric width strips cream tone-on-tone. Cut the strips into ten 6 1/2" segments for A and five 2" segments for B.

Step 2. Cut three 6 7/8" x 6 7/8" squares cream tone-on-tone; cut each square in half on one diagonal to make C triangles. You will need five C triangles.

Step 3. Cut three 3 7/8" x 3 7/8" squares cream tone-on-tone; cut each square in half on one diagonal to make D triangles. You will need five D triangles.

Step 4. Cut three 3 7/8" x 3 7/8" squares gold check; cut each square in half on one diagonal to make E triangles. You will need five E triangles.

Step 5. Cut five 2" x 2" squares dark green check for F.

Step 6. Cut one 2 3/8" x 22" strip gold check; subcut strip into 2 3/8" square segments. Cut each square in half on one diagonal to make G triangles. You will need 10 G triangles.

Step 7. Cut three 2 3/8" x 22" strips each dark green check and cream tone-on-tone.

Step 8. Lay a cream tone-on-tone strip right sides together with a dark green check strip, aligning edges perfectly; subcut into 2 3/8" square segments. Repeat with all strips. You will need 20 layered squares for H units.

Step 9. Draw a diagonal line from corner to corner on one side of each layered H unit. Sew 1/4" on each side of the marked line as shown in Figure 1. Cut on the diagonal line to make two H units as shown in Figure 2.

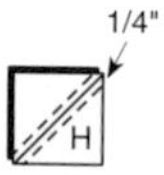

Figure 1
Draw a diagonal line from corner to corner on 1 side of each layered H unit. Sew 1/4" on each side of the marked line.

Figure 2
Cut on the diagonal line to make 2 H units.

Step 10. Cut two strips each 2 3/8" x 22" width gold and dark green checks. Repeat Steps 8 and 9 to make J units as shown in Figure 3; you will need 40 J units.

Figure 3
Make J units.

Step 11. To piece one block, join four H units as shown in Figure 4; repeat. Press seams in one direction. Sew B to the end of one unit, again referring to Figure 4; press seam toward H.

Step 12. Sew the H and B-H units to C as shown in Figure 5; press seams toward C.

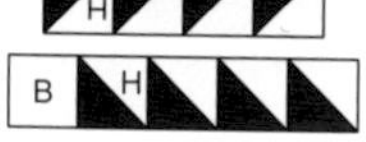

Figure 4
Join 4 H units as shown; repeat. Sew B to the end of 1 unit.

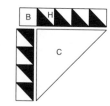

Figure 5
Sew the H and B-H units to C.

Step 13. Join two J units and add G as shown in Figure 6; repeat for two G-J units. Press seams in one direction. Sew F to the gold check end of one unit, again referring to Figure 6; press seams toward F.

Ruched Roses & Baskets
Placement Diagram
35 3/4" x 35 3/4"

Step 14. Sew the G-J and G-J-F units to E as shown in Figure 7; press seams toward E.

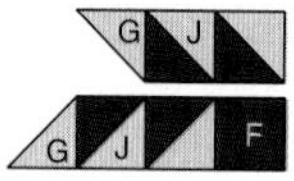

Figure 6
Join 2 J units and add G as shown; repeat for 2 G-J units. Sew F to the gold check end of 1 unit.

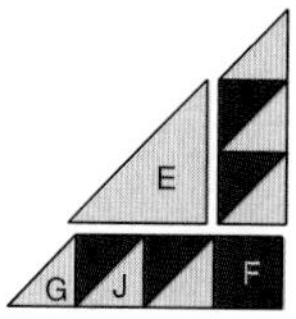

Figure 7
Sew the G-J and G-J-F units to E.

Step 15. Sew the G-J-F-E unit to the B-H-C unit as shown in Figure 8; press seam toward C.

Step 16. Sew G to A; repeat to make two A-G units as shown in Figure 9.

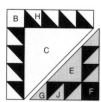

Figure 8
Sew the G-J-F-E unit to the B-H-C unit.

Figure 9
Sew G to A; repeat to make 2 A-G units.

Step 17. Sew the A-G units to the previously pieced unit and add D to complete one Rose Basket block as shown in Figure 10; press seams toward A-G and D. Repeat for five blocks.

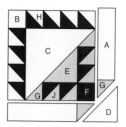

Figure 10
Sew the A-G units to the previously pieced unit and add D to complete 1 Rose Basket block.

Making Flowers

Step 1. Cut five 2 1/2" x 11" rectangles from each of the rose tone-on-tone fabrics.

Step 2. Fold each rectangle with wrong sides together to make a 1 1/4" x 11" strip.

Step 3. Using a double, knotted strand of matching thread, and starting on one end of the folded strip, stitch large gathering stitches in a large zigzag design down the entire length of the fabric as shown in Figure 11.

Figure 11
Stitch large gathering stitches in a large zigzag design down the entire length of the fabric.

Step 4. Pull the gathering stitches to create a folded woven shape as shown in Figure 12. Pull the same gathering thread to form a circle of the shape as shown in Figure 13; tack the ends of the circle together to make a ruched rose. Repeat for five ruched roses in each color.

Figure 12
Pull the gathering stitches to create a folded woven shape.

Figure 13
Pull the same gathering thread to form a circle of the shape.

Finishing Blocks

Step 1. Prepare template for leaf shape; cut as directed on the piece, adding a 1/8"–1/4" seam allowance all around when cutting.

Step 2. Turn under seam allowance on each leaf shape and position three leaves on one Rose Basket block as shown in Figure 14; hand-stitch in place using matching thread.

Figure 14
Position 3 leaves on 1
Rose Basket block.

Step 3. Position one ruched rose of each color over leaves; tuck the ends to the back and tack in place to secure. Repeat for five blocks.

Completing Quilt

Step 1. Cut one 9 1/2" by fabric width strip green tone-on-tone; subcut strip into 2" segments for K. You will need 16 K pieces for sashing.

Step 2. Cut four 2" x 2" squares (L) and four 2 3/8" x 2 3/8" squares (M) dark rose tone-on-tone. Cut the M squares in half on one diagonal to make M triangles; you will need eight M triangles.

Step 3. Cut one 14" x 14" square (N) and two 7 1/4" x 7 1/4" squares (O) cream tone-on-tone. Cut the N square in half on both diagonals to make N triangles and the O square in half on one diagonal to make O triangles.

Step 4. Join three Rose Basket blocks with four K strips and two O triangles to make the center row as shown in Figure 15; press seams toward K.

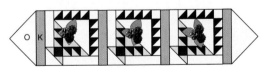

Figure 15
Join 3 Rose Basket blocks with 4 K strips
and 2 O triangles to make the center row.

Step 5. Join one Rose Basket block with two K strips and two N triangles to make a row as shown in Figure 16; repeat for two rows. Press seams toward K.

Step 6. Join one K strip and two M triangles to make a sashing row as shown in Figure 17; repeat. Join three K strips with two L squares and two M triangles to make a sashing row, again referring to Figure 17; repeat for two sashing rows. Press seams toward K.

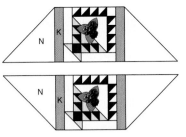

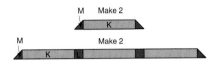

Figure 16
Join 1 Rose Basket block with 2 K
strips and 2 N triangles to make a row.

Figure 17
Make sashing rows as shown.

Step 7. Join the block rows with the sashing rows to complete the pieced center as shown in Figure 18; press seams toward K.

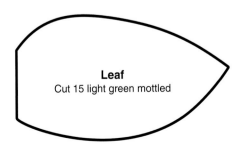

Figure 18
Join the block rows with the sashing
rows to complete the pieced center.

Step 8. Cut two strips each 3 1/2" x 30 1/4" and 3 1/2" x 36 1/4" dark green floral. Sew the shorter strips to opposite sides and longer strips to the top and bottom of the pieced center; press seams toward strips.

Step 9. Prepare for quilting and quilt as desired referring to the General Instructions. *Note: The project shown was machine-quilted in a meandering pattern in the cream tone-on-tone pieces using cream machine-quilting thread.*

Step 10. Prepare 4 1/2 yards dark rose tone-on-tone binding and apply referring to the General Instructions to finish. ❖

Leaf
Cut 15 light green mottled

Posy Patch

By Sue Harvey

Frayed edges form the petals in this garden of pastel posies.

Project Specifications

Skill Level: Beginner

Quilt Size: 56" x 72"

Block Size: 8" x 8"

Number of Blocks: 18

Materials

- 17 pastel 1930s print fat quarters
- 3 1/2 yards yellow print
- Batting 60" x 76"
- Backing 60" x 76"
- All-purpose thread to match fabrics
- Pastel-variegated machine-quilting thread
- 1 skein 6-strand yellow embroidery floss
- Basting spray
- Basic sewing tools and supplies, rotary cutter, mat and ruler, yo-yo template and embroidery needle

Instructions

Step 1. Cut four strips 8 1/2" by fabric width yellow print; subcut into 17 squares 8 1/2" x 8 1/2" for flower background squares.

Step 2. Cut two strips each 2 1/2" x 44 1/2", 2 1/2" x 56 1/2", 4 1/2" x 56 1/2" and 4 1/2" x 64 1/2" along remaining length of the yellow print; set aside for borders.

Step 3. Cut 36 squares 4 1/2" x 4 1/2" yellow print for A.

Step 4. From each pastel print fat quarter, cut two strips 2 1/2" x 22" and one strip 2 1/4" x 22"; set aside the 2 1/4" strips for binding.

Step 5. Join two randomly selected 2 1/2" strips along length to make a strip set; repeat to make 17 strip sets. Cut each strip set into 2 1/2" segments as shown in Figure 1.

Four-Patch
8" x 8" Block

Figure 1
Cut strip sets into
2 1/2" segments.

Figure 2
Join 2 segments
to make a
Four-Patch unit.

Step 6. Join two segments to make a Four-Patch unit as shown in Figure 2; repeat for 36 Four-Patch units. Set aside remaining segments for the pieced border.

Step 7. Sew an A square to one side of each Four-Patch unit as shown in Figure 3; press seams toward

Step 8. Join two pieced strips to complete one Four-Patch block as shown in Figure 4; repeat for 18 blocks.

Figure 3
Sew an A square to
a Four-Patch unit.

Figure 4
Complete 1 Four-Patch
block as shown.

Step 9. Trace one each 6 1/2", 4 1/2" and 2 1/2" circles on one pastel print fat quarter using the purchased yo-yo template. ***Note:*** *If not using a purchased yo-yo template, make a template for each size circle.*

Step 10. Cut out the circles to form flower shapes as shown in Figure 5; repeat with all pastel print fat quarters.

Step 11. Lightly apply basting spray to the wrong side of a 6 1/2" flower shape; center it on a flower background square and smooth in place. Repeat to center a 4 1/2" flower shape and a 2 1/2" flower shape on the larger flower shape as shown in Figure 6, using a different print for each size.

Figure 5
Cut out circles
to form flower
shapes.

Figure 6
Place flower
shapes on a
background square
as shown.

Step 12. Repeat Step 11 to make 17 flower units.

Step 13. Using pastel-variegated machine-quilting thread in the top of the machine and all-purpose thread in the bobbin, topstitch 1/2" inside the edge of each flower shape as shown in Figure 7.

Step 14. Join two flower units with three Four-Patch blocks to make a row as shown in Figure 8; repeat for four rows.

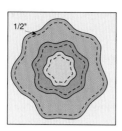

Figure 7
Topstitch 1/2" inside
the edge of each
flower shape.

Step 15. Join three flower units with two Four-Patch blocks to make a row, again referring to Figure 8; repeat for three rows.

Make 3

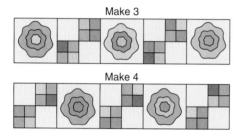

Make 4

Figure 8
Join flower units and blocks to make rows.

Step 16. Join the rows to complete the pieced center referring to the Placement Diagram for positioning of rows.

Step 17. Sew the 2 1/2" x 56 1/2" yellow print border strips to opposite long sides of the pieced center and the 2 1/2" x 44 1/2" yellow print border strips to the top and bottom; press seams toward strips.

Step 18. Join 15 segments set aside in Step 6 to make a border strip as shown in Figure 9; repeat. Sew a strip to opposite long sides of the pieced center.

Figure 9
Join segments to make border strips.

Step 19. Join 12 segments to make a border strip, again referring to Figure 9; repeat. Sew a strip to the top and bottom of the pieced center.

Step 20. Sew the 4 1/2" x 64 1/2" yellow print border strips to opposite long sides of the pieced center and the 4 1/2" x 56 1/2" strips to the top and bottom to complete the top; press seams toward strips.

Step 21. Prepare for quilting and quilt referring to the General Instructions. ***Note:** The sample shown was professionally machine-quilted.*

Step 22. Trim edges even. Join the 2 1/4" binding strips set aside in Step 4 on short ends to make a long

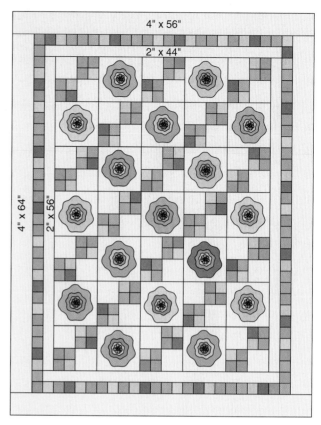

Posy Patch
Placement Diagram
56" x 72"

strip as shown in Figure 10. Press strip in half along length with wrong sides together; bind edges of quilt referring to the General Instructions.

Step 23. Cut a 2 1/2" circle from each pastel print fat quarter. Hand- or machine-baste 1/2" inside the edge of each circle using pastel-variegated machine-quilting thread; pull thread to draw edge tightly to the center, knot thread and flatten to make a yo-yo, leaving the raw edge exposed at top of yo-yo as shown in Figure 11.

Figure 10
Join binding
strips on short
ends as shown.

Figure 11
Make a yo-yo, leaving
the raw edge exposed.

Step 24. Use a 6" length of 6-strand yellow embroidery floss to attach a yo-yo to the center of each flower, bringing the ends of the embroidery floss up through the center of the yo-yo and knotting tightly; trim ends 1/8"–1/4" beyond yo-yo.

Step 25. Wash and dry quilt to fray edges of flowers. ❖

Flowers & Grapes Baskets

By Pearl Louise Krush

Fabric yo-yos make the grapes, and folded squares create the petals on this basket-design wall quilt.

Project Specifications

Skill Level: Beginner

Quilt Size: 14" x 34"

Block Size: 10" x 10"

Number of Blocks: 3

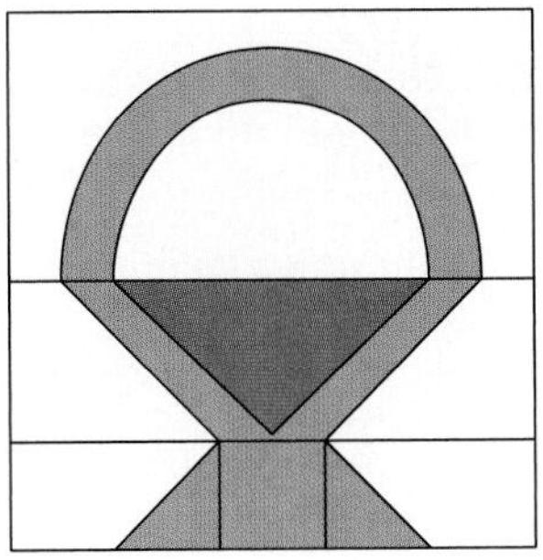

Materials

- 1 fat quarter pink print
- 1 fat quarter green print
- 1 fat quarter dark green mottled
- 1 fat quarter each 2 different burgundy tone-on-tones
- 2 fat quarters tan print
- 1/2 yard burgundy print
- 1/2 yard cream-on-cream print
- Backing 18" x 38"
- Batting 18" x 38"
- All-purpose thread to match fabrics
- Cream machine-quilting thread
- Basic sewing tools and supplies, rotary cutter, mat and ruler

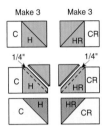

Basket
12" x 12" Block

Instructions

Making Basket Blocks

Step 1. Cut six rectangles each 2 1/2" x 4 1/2" for B and 3 1/2" x 4 1/2" for C, and three rectangles 5 1/2" x 10 1/2" for D from cream-on-cream print.

Step 2. Cut nine 2 1/2" x 2 1/2" squares tan print for A and G. Cut six 3 1/2" x 3 1/2" squares tan print for H. Cut three 2 1/2" x 3 1/2" rectangles tan print for J. Draw a diagonal line from corner to corner on the wrong side of each G and H square.

Step 3. To piece one Basket block, lay a G square right sides together with B referring to Figure 1; stitch on the diagonal line. Trim seam to 1/4"; press G to the right side. Repeat for three B-G and three BR-GR units, again referring to Figure 1.

Step 4. Lay an H square right sides together with C referring to Figure 2; stitch on the diagonal line. Trim seam to 1/4"; press H to the right side. Repeat for three C-H and three CR-HR units, again referring to Figure 2.

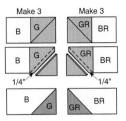

Figure 1
Lay a G square right sides together with B; stitch on the diagonal line. Trim seam to 1/4"; press G to the right side.

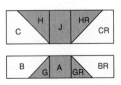

Figure 2
Lay an H square right sides together with C; stitch on the diagonal line. Trim seam to 1/4"; press H to the right side.

Step 5. Sew an A square between one B-G and one BR-GR unit as shown in Figure 3. Repeat with J between the C-H and CR-HR units, again referring to Figure 3.

Step 6. Join the pieced units as shown in Figure 4.

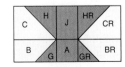

Figure 3
Sew an A square between 1 B-G and 1 BR-GR unit as shown; repeat with J between the C-H and CR-HR units.

Figure 4
Join the pieced units as shown.

Step 7. Cut two squares green print 4 1/2" x 4 1/2"; cut each square on one diagonal to make F triangles. You will need three F triangles.

Flowers & Grapes Basket
Placement Diagram
14" x 34"

Step 8. Turn under both short edges of F 1/4" and press. Center F on J as shown in Figure 5; baste in place along raw edge and hand-stitch short folded edges to the pieced unit.

Step 9. Prepare template for the E basket handle piece given on page 139; cut as directed on the piece. Turn under curved edges 1/4"; press. Hand-stitch E to D, placing edge of E 1 1/2" from outer edges as shown in Figure 6.

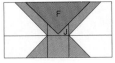

Figure 5
Center F on J.

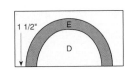

Figure 6
Hand-stitch E to D, placing edge
of E 1 1/2" from outer edges.

Step 10. Sew the D-E unit to the C-J-J-F edge of the previously pieced unit referring to Figure 7 to complete one Basket block; repeat for three Basket blocks and press.

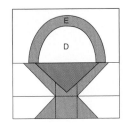

Figure 7
Sew the D-E unit to the C-J-J-F
edge of the previously pieced unit.

Making Yo-Yo Grapes & Flower Centers

Step 1. Prepare template for yo-yo circle using pattern given; cut as directed on the piece.

Step 2. Fold 1/8" to the wrong side of one circle and using a double, knotted matching thread and a hand-sewing needle, sew larger gathering stitches around folded edge as shown in Figure 8.

Figure 8
Make yo-yo as shown.

Step 3. Pull the gathering stitches tight to pull edges to the center; tie off to complete one yo-yo, again referring to Figure 8. Repeat for 69 burgundy tone-on-tone and six cream-on-cream print yo-yos.

Making Petal Flowers & Buds

Step 1. Cut 39 squares pink print and three squares dark green mottled 2 1/2" x 2 1/2".

Step 2. Fold each square in half with wrong sides together on the diagonal. Using a double, knotted matching thread, and starting on one raw edge of the folded square, stitch large gathering stitches to the other folded edge as shown in Figure 9.

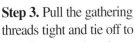

Figure 9
Fold each square in half with wrong sides together on the diagonal. Using a double, knotted matching thread, and starting on 1 folded corner of the folded square, stitch large gathering stitches to the other folded corner.

Step 3. Pull the gathering threads tight and tie off to complete a petal as shown in Figure 10; repeat for 39 petals.

Step 4. Sew five petals onto a double, knotted matching thread as shown in Figure 11; pull the petals close together and form a circle. Secure the first and last petals together to make a five-petal flower.

Figure 10
Pull the gathering threads tight and tie off to complete a petal.

Figure 11
Sew 5 petals onto a double, knotted matching thread; pull petals close to form a circle.

Step 5. To make buds, join three petals as in Step 4.

Step 6. Fold a 2 1/2" x 2 1/2" square dark green mottled in half with wrong sides together on the diagonal. Fold the folded edge around the bud bottom, overlapping and trimming to fit on the bud back. Tack the fabric in place to cover the bud bottom referring to Figure 12.

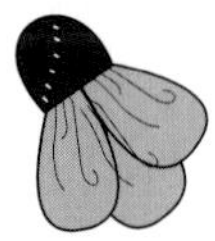

Figure 12
Tack the fabric in place to cover the bud bottom.

Finishing

Step 1. Prepare template for leaf shape using pattern given on page 139; cut as directed on the piece, adding a 1/8"–1/4" seam allowance all around when cutting.

Step 2. Turn under raw edges of each leaf and baste to hold.

Step 3. Arrange two leaves with one petal flower and a cluster of six to eight burgundy tone-on-tone yo-yos on a Basket block referring to Figure 13. Repeat with one bud, one leaf, one petal flower and another cluster of burgundy tone-on-tone yo-yos on the opposite side, again referring to Figure 13.

Step 4. Tack pieces in place by hand; sew a cream-on-cream print yo-yo to the center of each petal flower to complete the block. Repeat for three blocks.

Step 5. Join the three Basket blocks referring to the Placement Diagram for positioning; press seams in one direction.

Step 6. Cut two strips each 2 1/2" x 14 1/2" and 2 1/2" x 30 1/2" burgundy print. Sew the longer strips to

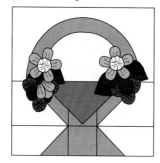

Figure 13
Arrange 2 leaves with 1 petal flower and a cluster of 6 to 8 burgundy tone-on-tone yo-yos on a basket block. Repeat with 1 bud, 1 leaf, 1 petal flower and another cluster of burgundy tone-on-tone yo-yos on the opposite side.

opposite sides and shorter strips to the top and bottom of the pieced center; press seams toward strips.

Step 7. Create 1 1/4 yards 1/4"-wide bias from dark green mottled. Cut into one 14 1/2" and one 24 1/2" length for vine pieces. Turn in each end of each piece 1/4"; hand-stitch closed.

Step 8. Arrange the 14 1/2" vine piece, three leaves and a cluster of eight burgundy tone-on-tone yo-yos on the bottom corner referring to Figure 14; hand-stitch pieces in place using thread to match fabric.

Step 9. Arrange the 24 1/2" vine piece with three leaves and two burgundy tone-on-tone yo-yo clusters of six, and one cluster of eight referring to Figure 15; hand-stitch pieces in place using thread to match fabrics.

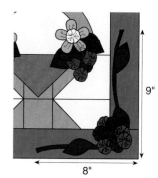

Figure 14
Arrange the 14 1/2" vine piece, 3 leaves and a cluster of 8 burgundy tone-on-tone yo-yos on the bottom corner.

Figure 15
Arrange the 24 1/2" vine piece, 3 leaves and 2 burgundy tone-on-tone yo-yo clusters of 6, and 1 cluster of 8 as shown.

Step 10. Prepare for quilting and quilt as desired referring to the General Instructions. ***Note:*** *The project shown was machine quilted in a meandering pattern in the cream-on-cream print pieces using cream machine-quilting thread.*

Step 11. Prepare 3 1/4 yards burgundy print binding and apply referring to the General Instructions to finish. ❖

Patterns continued on page 139

The Earth Laughs in Flowers

By Chris Malone

Decorate a metal tin with patchwork 3-D flowers and appliqué motifs.

Project Specifications

Skill Level: Intermediate

Project Size: 32 1/4" x 10 1/2"

Lid Size: 32 1/4" x 10 1/2" side cover and 10" diameter lide cover

Materials

- 1 fat quarter each green and pink florals
- 1 fat quarter green plaid
- Coordinating fabric scraps as follows: muslin or light tan print, two blue prints, 3 different shades gold print, 2–3 shades rose print, 2–4 green prints, white print, tan print, brown check and black solid
- 1/3 yard coordinating fabric for backing
- Batting 32 3/4" x 11" for side and 12" x 24" for lid
- All-purpose thread to match fabrics
- Ecru hand-quilting thread
- Dark brown and dark green 6-strand embroidery floss
- Metal popcorn tin 11" high and 10" diameter with lid
- 2 yards 7/8"-wide pink grosgrain ribbon
- 4 (7/8") any-color shank buttons for sunflower centers
- 1 (5/8") any-color shank button for rabbit tail
- 5 (5/8") black shank buttons
- 3 (7/8") pink buttons
- 1 (5/8") dark blue bird novelty button
- 3mm black bead
- 1 yard 3/4"-wide ecru braid trim
- 1 yard 1 1/4"-wide ecru Cluny lace
- 1/8 yard fusible transfer web
- Basic sewing tools and supplies, fabric glue, fade-out pen, pencil, embroidery needle and hoop

Instructions

Step 1. Draw a 5 1/2" x 5 1/2" square on the scrap of muslin or light tan print with a pencil. Transfer the message given to the center of the square using the fade-out pen.

Step 2. Place the marked fabric in the embroidery hoop and backstitch words using 2 strands dark brown embroidery floss on the large letters and 1 strand on the name. Make French knots on letters using 2 strands

dark brown embroidery floss. Cut out the square on the marked line.

Step 3. For remaining sections, cut a 3 1/4" x 5 1/2" piece blue print for A birdhouse; one 3 1/4" x 5 1/2" piece green print for B rabbit; one 5 3/4" x 5 3/4" square green floral for C yo-yo flowers; one 5 3/4" x 5 3/4" square green plaid for D ruched flowers; one 5 1/2" x 7 1/2" piece blue print for E sunflowers; and a 4" x 15" strip pink floral for F gathered section.

Step 4. For rabbit and birdhouse blocks, trace patterns given onto the paper side of the fusible transfer web; cut out just outside traced lines.

Step 5. Iron traced shapes onto the wrong side of fabrics as directed on the pieces for color. Cut out shapes on traced lines; remove paper backing.

Step 6. Arrange the rabbit shape on B and the birdhouse shapes on A as shown in Figure 1, with birdhouse roofs overlapping top of house pieces as indicated on patterns; fuse shapes in place.

Step 7. Draw several blades of grass near rabbit's feet using fade-out pen; stem-stitch over lines using 3 strands dark green embroidery floss.

Step 8. Sew the bottom edge of B to the top edge of the message square; sew A to the bottom of the message square to complete the A-B panel as shown in Figure 2. Press seams away from the message square.

Step 9. Prepare ruched flower centers and two stems using fusible transfer web as in Steps 4 and 5, and arrange on the D square referring to Figure 3 for positioning; fuse in place. Trim excess pieces at bottom.

Figure 2
Sew the bottom edge of B to the top edge of the message square; sew A to the bottom of the message square to complete the A-B panel.

Figure 1
Arrange the rabbit shape on B and the birdhouse shapes on A.

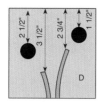

Figure 3
Arrange stems and flower
centers on the D square.

Step 10. To make ruched flowers, cut one bias strip each 1 1/4" x 12" and one 1 1/4" x 14" rose print. Fold under 1/4" along one long raw edge of each strip for hem and press. Fold opposite long raw edge down almost to bottom of hem and press as shown in Figure 4.

Figure 4
Fold under 1/4" along 1 long raw
edge of each strip for hem and
press. Fold opposite long raw edge
down almost to bottom of hem.

Step 11. Referring to Figure 5 and beginning 1/2" in from one end of each strip, mark dots 1" apart across the folded top edge. Mark dots 1" apart along the bottom edges, starting 1" in from the end of the strip, again referring to Figure 5.

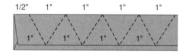

Figure 5
Beginning 1/2" in from 1 end of each
strip, mark dots 1" apart across the top
edge. Mark dots 1" apart along the
bottom edges, starting 1" in from the
end of the strip. Hand-stitch a running
stitch from the first dot at the top edge
to the first dot at the bottom edge.

Step 12. Using matching all-purpose thread, hand-stitch a running stitch from the first dot at the top edge to the first dot at the bottom edge, again referring to Figure 5. Continue sewing in a zigzag path, gathering as you sew and ending at the last dot on the top edge; knot thread to hold gathers. The shorter strip should measure approximately 4 1/2" along length and the longer strip about 5 1/2" along length.

Step 13. Fold each ruched strip in half, right sides together, and join short ends to form a circle as shown in Figure 6.

Step 14. Position each circle around a fused flower center; hand-stitch gathers in place. Tack each petal end in place.

Figure 6
Fold each ruched strip in half,
right sides together, and join
short ends to form a circle.

Step 15. To make prairie points for grass, cut four 3" x 3" squares green print. Fold each square in half on the diagonal, then in half again as shown in Figure 7; press. Evenly arrange the four folded triangles along the bottom of D as shown in Figure 8, overlapping as necessary; baste in place to hold.

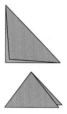

Figure 7
Fold each square in half on the
diagonal, then in half again.

Figure 8
Evenly arrange the 4 folded
triangles along the bottom of D.

Step 16. Sew D to C, catching the raw edge of the prairie point triangles in the seam as shown in Figure 9; press seam toward C.

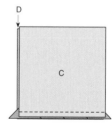

Figure 9
Sew D to C, catching the
raw edge of the prairie point
triangles in the seam.

Step 17. For the gathered block, sew gathering stitches 1/4" from each long edge of F as shown in Figure 10. Sew a second line 1/8" from edge. Pull threads to gather edges on the top and bottom until F is 5 1/2" wide, leaving 1/4" on each short side ungathered referring to Figure 11.

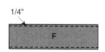

Figure 10
Sew gathering
stitches 1/4" from
each long edge of F.

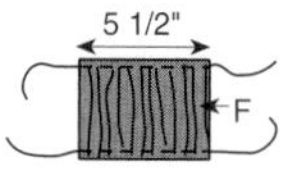

Figure 11
Pull threads to gather edges
on the top and bottom until F
is 5 1/2" wide, leaving 1/4" on
each short side ungathered.

the earth
laughs
in flowers

Thoreau

Step 18. Sew through gathers along one side to stabilize edge; sew other gathered edge to one short side of E as shown in Figure 12. Press seam toward E.

Figure 12
Sew 1 gathered edge
to 1 short side of E.

Step 19. Prepare two stems (one trimmed about 1 1/2" shorter than the other) using fusible transfer web as in Steps 4 and 5, and fuse to E referring to Figure 13.

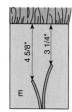

Figure 13
Fuse stems to E.

Step 20. Sew the E-F unit to the right side edge of A-B as shown in Figure 14; press seam toward E-F. Sew C-D to the left side edge of A-B, again referring to Figure 14; press seam toward C-D.

Figure 14
Sew E-F and C-D to A-B as shown;
press seams away from A-B.

Step 21. Cut one 9" x 11" rectangle each green floral (G) and pink floral (H); sew to the pieced panel as shown in Figure 15. Press seams toward G and H.

The Earth Laughs in Flowers
Placement Diagram
32 1/4" x 10 1/2"

Figure 15
Sew G and H to the pieced panel.

Step 22. Cut 7/8"-wide pink grosgrain ribbon into six 12" lengths; pin three ribbons to each short end of the pieced top, one in the center and the remaining lengths 1/2" from top and bottom edges as shown in Figure 16. Baste to secure.

Figure 16
Pin ribbon to panel as shown.

Step 23. Cut an 11" x 32 3/4" rectangle from backing fabric. Place the batting piece on a flat surface; lay the backing right side up on batting. Place the pieced-and-appliquéd top right side down on the backing; pin layers together.

Step 24. Stitch around all sides of the layered unit, leaving a 6" opening on the bottom near one corner; clip corners and trim batting close to seam. Turn right side out through opening; press. Hand-stitch opening closed.

Step 25. Quilt as desired by hand or machine. *Note: The sample was hand-quilted in the ditch of seams between pieces using ecru hand-quilting thread.*

Step 26. To finish yo-yo flower C square, cut fabric circles referring to pattern. Fold and finger-press a 1/8" hem around each circle edge. Hand-sew gathering stitches all around with a doubled strand of knotted thread; pull thread to gather lightly as shown in Figure 17. Use fingers to move the small opening to the center to make a yo-yo flower.

Step 27. Sew a 5/8" black button to the center of each yo-yo flower as shown in Figure 18.

Step 28. Center and sew three yo-yo flowers on C, sewing through buttons to secure.

Step 29. Cut three 4" x 4" squares green print for leaves. Fold each square in half to make a 2" x 4" rectangle. Fold each top corner down to the center bottom of the rectangle as shown in Figure 19; press. Hand-sew gathering stitches across raw edge; pull to gather bottom of leaf as shown in Figure 20. Repeat for three leaves.

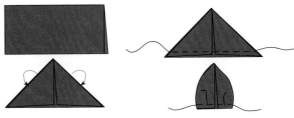

Figure 19
Fold each top corner down to th center bottom of the rectangle

Figure 20
Hand-sew gathering stitches across raw edge; pull to gather bottom of leaf.

Step 30. Tack or glue bottom of each leaf under edges of yo-yo flowers as shown in Figure 21 to finish C.

Step 31. To finish E, draw seven sunflower petals on the wrong side of one gold print, leaving about 3/8" between petals. Place the marked fabric over another piece of the same fabric with right sides together; sew on the traced lines, leaving bottom edge unstitched as shown in Figure 22. Repeat with second gold print.

Figure 21
Tack or glue bottom of each leaf under edges as shown.

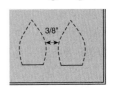

Figure 22
Place the marked fabric over another piece of fabric with right sides together; sew on the traced lines, leaving bottom edge unstitched.

Figure 17
Make yo-yo flowers as shown.

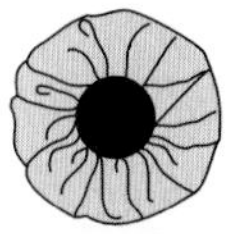

Figure 18
Sew a black button to the center of each yo-yo flower.

Step 32. Cut petals about 1/8" from seam, clip corners and turn right side out. Hand-sew gathering stitches along bottom of one petal; pull to gather. Gather another same-fabric petal on the same thread referring to Figure 23. Continue to add petals until seven are connected; join the first and last petals to make a circular flower as shown in Figure 24. Repeat to make a second flower.

Figure 23
Hand-sew gathering
stitches along bottom
of 1 petal; pull to gather
and pick up another petal.

Figure 24
Continue to add petals
until 7 are connected;
join the first and last petals
together to make a
circular flower.

Step 33. Cut sunflower center pieces as directed on pattern. Hand-sew gathering stitches around edge of center circles; place a 7/8" shank button, round side down, on center of wrong side of circle; pull thread to gather fabric around shank. Knot thread; then push shank through center of flower and sew flower center to E on stem piece, sewing through all layers. Repeat with remaining flower.

Step 34. In the same manner, cover 5/8" shank button with white print using circle pattern given for rabbit tail and sew to rabbit for tail. Sew 3mm black bead to face for eye.

Step 35. Evenly space and sew three 7/8" pink buttons to top of F as shown in Figure 25.

Step 36. Sew 5/8" dark blue bird button to birdhouse A section.

Figure 25
Evenly space and
sew 3 pink buttons
to top of F.

Step 37. To cover the top of tin, place lid on wrong side of green plaid and draw around with pencil; measure 3/4" out from circle and draw a new pattern and cut out. Cut two circles from batting; glue one batting circle to lid and glue second circle on top of first.

Step 38. Hand-sew large gathering stitches around edge of fabric circle. Place fabric over padded top of lid, right side up. Working a quarter of the lid at a time, gently pull thread to ease fabric and glue edge to side of lid.

Step 39. Apply glue to top right-side edge of Cluny lace; place bottom wrong-side edge of braid trim on glued edge. Glue trim to side of lid with lace extending below edge of lid.

Step 40. To decorate lid, make two sunflowers referring to Steps 31–33 and two yo-yo flowers from rose and blue prints, and four leaves from green print as directed in Steps 26–30. Arrange and glue to top of lid referring to the Placement Diagram for positioning.

Step 41. Place patchwork section around metal tin; tie grosgrain ribbon bows to hold in place. Place lid on tin to finish. ❖

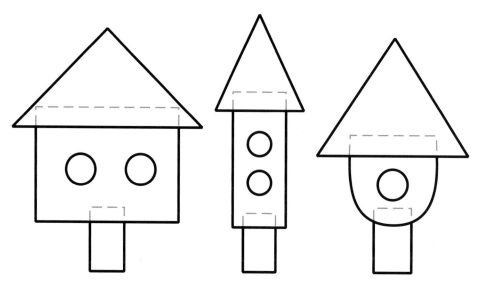

Birdhouses
Cut as follows: roofs—brown check; houses—tan print; poles—brown check; & openings—black solid

Yo-Yo Circle
Cut 1 gold print & 2 each
rose & blue prints

Sunflower Petal
Cut 28 each 2
gold prints

Sunflower Center
Cut 4 gold
print

Rabbit
Cut 1 white print

X

**Rabbit Tail &
Ruched Flower Center**
Cut 1 white print &
2 dark rose print

Stem
Cut 4 green print

the earth
laughs
in flowers
thoreau

Message

Gather Ye Roses

By Barbara A. Clayton

Fabric roses are the focal point on this pretty decorator pillow.

Project Specifications

Skill Level: Intermediate

Pillow Size: 20" x 20"

Materials

- Scraps or 1/8 yard maroon solid
- Scraps or 1/8 yard cranberry solid
- Scraps or 1/8 yard 2 medium rose prints
- Scraps or 1/8 yard dark green solid
- Scraps or 1/8 yard dark green print
- 3 fat quarters or 1 yard muslin
- 4 fat quarters or 1 yard dark blue print
- Batting 14" x 14"
- All-purpose thread to match fabrics
- Blue hand-quilting thread
- 1/8 yard medium-weight fusible interfacing
- 2 1/3 yards 1/2" cotton cord
- 20" x 20" pillow form
- Heavy fishing line
- Basic sewing tools and supplies and water-erasable marker or pencil, stylet, zipper foot and tape

Instructions

Completing Pillow Top

Step 1. Prepare templates using patterns given; cut as directed on each piece.

Step 2. Turn under edge of each A circle a scant 1/4"; sew all around edge with a double, knotted thread. Pull thread to gather the center to make yo-yo shapes as shown in Figure 1. Flatten to form small round circles; tie the thread and cut.

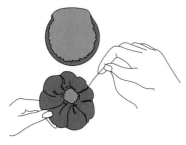

Figure 1
Make yo-yo centers as shown.

Step 3. Cut a 14" x 14" square muslin for background and one for lining; set the lining piece aside.

Step 4. Transfer the quilting design given on page 135 to the background square 2" from edge all around using the pattern given and a water-erasable marker or pencil.

Step 5. Pin a B piece to each C along the straight side with right sides together; stitch as shown in Figure 2. Press seams toward C.

Step 6. Pin the curved edges with right sides together with the first seam about 1/4" down from the folded edge as shown in Figure 3; stitch, leaving a 2" opening for turning. Clip points and curves and turn right side out. Slipstitch the opening closed.

Figure 2
Pin a B piece to each C along the straight side with right sides together; stitch as shown.

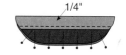

Figure 3
Pin the curved edges with right sides together with the first seam about 1/4" down from the folded edge.

Step 7. With a double strand of matching thread, sew a long running stitch along the curved seam and pull to gather slightly as shown in Figure 4. Hand-stitch the curved end of one side to the other curved end, overlapping about 1" as shown in Figure 5.

Figure 4
With a double strand of matching thread, sew a long running stitch along the curved seam and pull to gather slightly.

Figure 5
Hand-stitch the curved end of 1 side to the other curved end, overlapping about 1".

Step 8. Flatten the rose center and tuck a cranberry solid yo-yo (A) in the center of each rose as shown in Figure 6; hand-stitch in place.

Step 9. Fold each D petal in half along length with wrong sides together; hand-stitch a long gathering stitch along the open edge. Pull the thread to gather tightly; knot to secure.

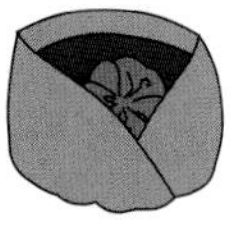

Figure 6
Flatten the rose
center and tuck a
cranberry solid yo-
yo in the center of
each rose.

Step 10. Place two medium rose print 2 petals directly under each rose center as shown in Figure 7; hand-stitch petals to the backside of the rose center. Repeat in the center with one medium rose print 1 petal as shown in Figure 8. Stitch two cranberry solid petals on each side of the center petal, again referring to Figure 8. Repeat for three rose flower/petal motifs; set aside.

Figure 7
Place 2 medium rose
print 2 petals directly
under each rose center.

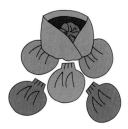

Figure 8
Sew 1 petal in the
center; sew a petal
on each side of the
center petal.

Step 11. Trace 10 leaf shapes onto the smooth side of the medium-weight fusible interfacing. Cut out leaf shapes leaving at least 1/4" beyond traced lines.

Step 12. Pin the interfacing leaves with the glue side to the right side of the fabrics, pinning five to the green solid and five to the green print. Stitch all around each leaf shape. Trim away excess fabric to 1/8", clipping curves and trimming points.

Step 13. Cut a small slit in the interfacing side of each leaf; turn right side out, running a stylet all around the seam on the inside to smooth. Transfer vein lines to each leaf.

Step 14. Cut three 1" x 5" bias strips from dark green solid; fold the raw edges of the bias in 1/4" on both sides and press. Fold the folded bias strips in half along length to make 1/4"-wide stem pieces.

Step 15. Fold the E pieces in half along length with wrong sides together and pin; repeat with F pieces. Lay an F piece on an E piece, about 1/8" down from the folded edge as shown in Figure 9.

Figure 9
Lay an F piece on an E piece, about
1/8" down from the folded edge.

Step 16. Fold both ends toward the center, overlapping slightly as shown in Figure 10. Fold raw bottom edge under about 1/4" as shown in Figure 11; pin.

Figure 10
Fold both ends toward the
center, overlapping slightly.

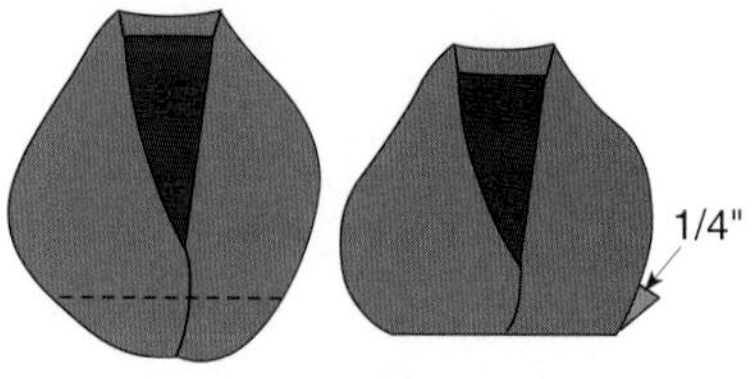

Figure 11
Fold raw bottom edge under
about 1/4" as shown.

Step 17. Fold both sides under diagonally as shown in Figure 12; pin to create a rosebud. Repeat for three rosebuds.

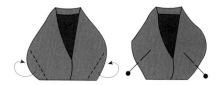

Figure 12
Fold both sides under diagonally
and pin to create a rosebud.

Gather Ye Roses
Placement Diagram
20" x 20"

Step 18. To make rosebud leaves, fold G piece in half along length with right sides together; stitch, leaving a 1 1/2" opening to turn. Clip points and curves; turn right side out. Slipstitch opening closed.

Step 19. Sew a running stitch through the center of each G; gather to make two small leaves as shown in Figure 13.

Step 20. Hand-stitch the gathered G piece to the bottom and sides of each rosebud as shown in Figure 14.

Figure 13
Sew a running stitch through the center of each G; gather to make 2 small leaves.

Figure 14
Hand-stitch the gathered G piece to the bottom and sides of each rosebud.

Step 21. Referring to the Placement Diagram, arrange stem pieces in the center of the marked background square; hand-stitch in place using matching thread.

Step 22. Arrange and hand-stitch a rosebud to the outside ends of each stem piece.

Step 23. Arrange leaves on the stems, again referring to the Placement Diagram for positioning; hand-stitch in place using matching thread.

Step 24. Hand-stitch the roses in place referring to the Placement Diagram for positioning.

Finishing Pillow

Step 1. Sandwich the batting between the appliquéd top and the lining square set aside in Step 3; pin or baste layers together. Hand-quilt on marked lines using blue hand-quilting thread. When quilting is complete, trim quilted square to 12 1/2" x 12 1/2", centering the quilting motif; remove pins or basting.

Step 2. Cut a 20 1/2" x 20 1/2" square dark blue print for pillow back; cut a same-size square muslin for lining. Layer with wrong sides together; set aside.

Step 3. Cut three 4 1/2" by fabric width strips dark blue print if using yardage or six 4 1/2" x 22" strips if using fat quarters. Join the strips on the short ends to make a tube.

Step 4. Zigzag with a medium-width and very long zigzag stitch over the heavy fishing line along both edges of the dark blue print tube within the 1/4" seam allowance as shown in Figure 15. Pull the heavy fishing line to gather evenly on one edge and pin to the quilted block right sides together. Clip in 1/4" at each corner to turn. Stitch in place; remove heavy fishing line from inside seam.

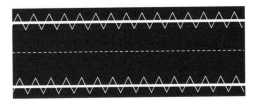

Figure 15
Zigzag with a medium-width and very long zigzag stitch over the heavy fishing line along both edges of the blue print tube within the 1/4" seam allowance.

Step 5. Cut two strips each 4 1/2" x 12 1/2" and 4 1/2" x 20 1/2" muslin. Sew the two short strips to the back of the quilted block on two opposite sides with a 1/4" seam. Repeat on the remaining sides with the longer strips. *Note: These strips become the stable edge for the outside gathered edge of the blue print strip.*

Step 6. Gather the remaining edge of the dark blue print tube as in Step 4; adjust gathers and pin to the muslin stabilizer strips. Round corners as shown in Figure 16; baste in place.

Step 7. Cut 2 1/4"-wide bias strips from dark blue print and join on short ends to make an 85" strip.

Step 8. Cover the 1/2"-wide cotton cord with the bias strip using a zipper foot as shown in Figure 17, starting stitching about 4" from beginning and stitch to within 4" of the end.

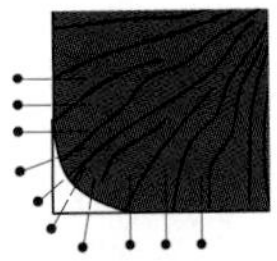

Figure 16
Round corners as shown

Zipper foot

Figure 17
Cover the 1/2"-wide cotton cord with the bias strip using a zipper foot.

Step 9. Pin the raw edges of the covered cord to the pillow top and stitch except for the beginning and ending 4".

Step 10. Mark where the cord ends will meet. Wrap tape around the mark on each end of the cord and cut the excess cord. Measure where the bias strip ends will meet and add 1/4" seam allowances on both ends. Trim away the excess bias strip; sew the bias ends together. Cover the remainder of the cord and stitch to the pillow top.

Step 11. Pin the layered backing/lining square right sides together with the finished pillow top; trim away rounded corners on backing/lining piece to match top. Sew all around, leaving a 10" opening on one side. Clip the curved corners and turn right side out.

Step 12. Insert the pillow form; slipstitch opening closed to finish. ❖

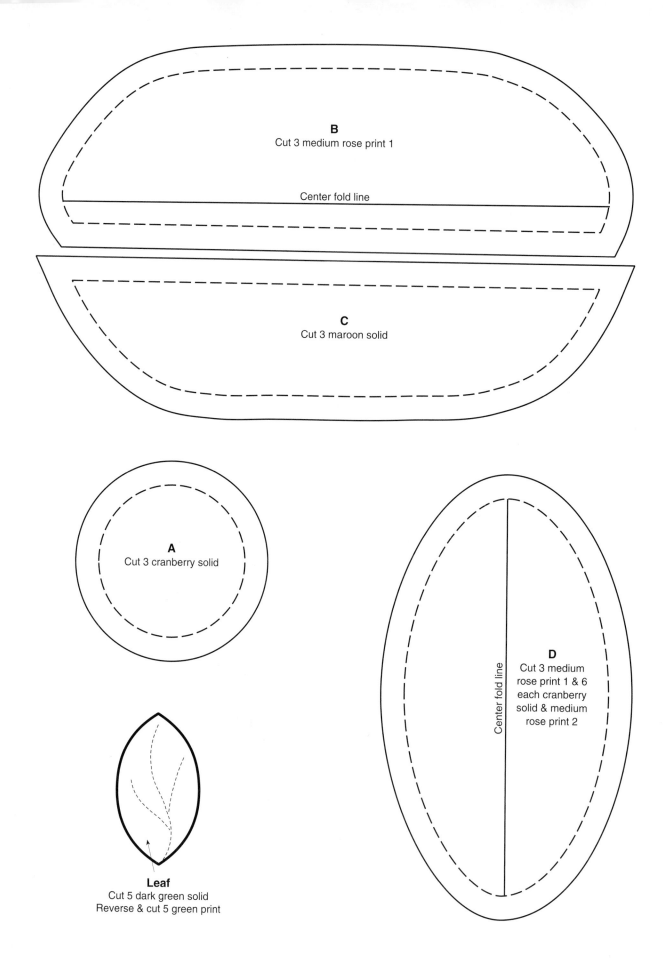

B
Cut 3 medium rose print 1

Center fold line

C
Cut 3 maroon solid

A
Cut 3 cranberry solid

Center fold line

D
Cut 3 medium
rose print 1 & 6
each cranberry
solid & medium
rose print 2

Leaf
Cut 5 dark green solid
Reverse & cut 5 green print

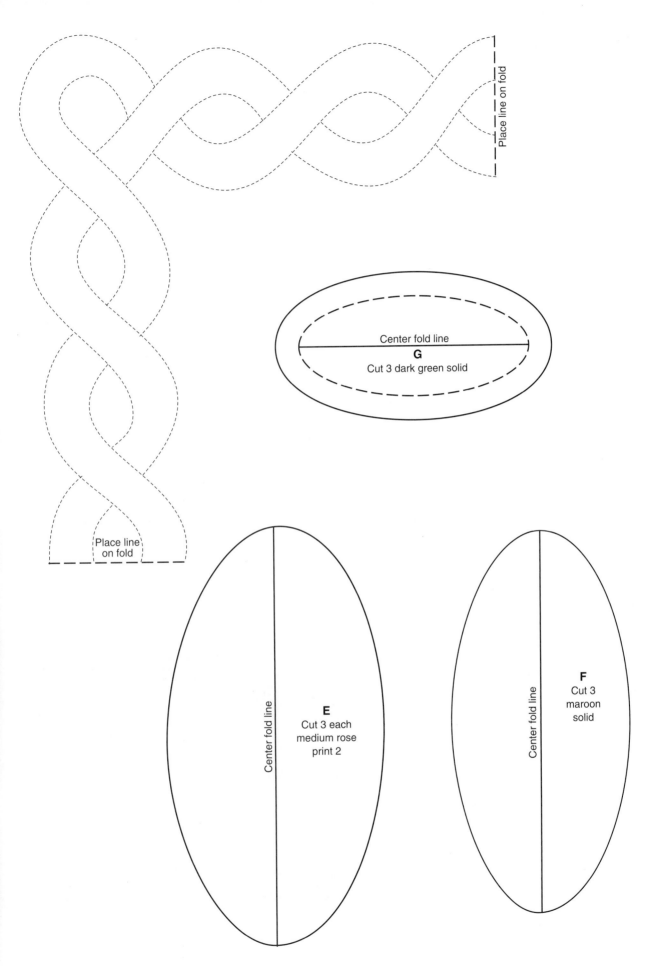

Place line on fold

Center fold line
G
Cut 3 dark green solid

Place line on fold

Center fold line

E
Cut 3 each
medium rose
print 2

Center fold line

F
Cut 3
maroon
solid

Petals & Leaves Pillow

By Marian Shenk

Appliquéd flowers and a pieced background create an interesting design on this corded pillow.

Project Specifications

Skill Level: Intermediate

Pillow Size: 17" x 17"

Materials

- 1 fat quarter cream-on-cream print
- 1 fat quarter red tone-on-tone
- 1 fat quarter green mottled
- 2 fat quarters red/green/white plaid
- Backing 18" x 18"
- Batting 18" x 18"
- All-purpose thread to match fabrics
- Cream hand-quilting thread
- 3/4 yard 3/8"-wide dark green bias tape
- Polyester fiberfill
- 1 1/4" button to cover
- 4 (3/4") gold buttons
- 2 1/4 yards 3/8" red cord with lip
- Basic sewing tools and supplies, zipper foot and water-erasable marker or pencil

Instructions

Step 1. Prepare templates using full-size drawing given for A, B and C and the pattern for D. Cut as directed on each piece, adding a 1/8"–1/4" seam allowance to A, B and C when cutting fabric patches.

Step 2. Cut six squares each cream-on-cream print and red/green/white plaid 4 1/2" x 4 1/2" for E.

Step 3. Cut two squares each cream-on-cream print and red/green/white plaid 7" x 7"; cut each square on both diagonals to make F triangles as shown in Figure 1.

Figure 1
Cut a 7" x 7" square
on both diagonals to
make F triangles.

Step 4. Join the E squares and F triangles in diagonal rows to complete the pieced background as shown in Figure 2.

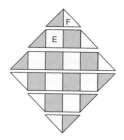

Figure 2
Join the E squares and F
triangles in diagonal rows to
complete the pieced background.

Step 5. Draw an 8" circle on the pieced background using a water-erasable marker or pencil. *Note: You may make the circle using the full-size quarter pattern given, using the edge of the bias as a guide to make the circle.*

Step 6. Turn under edges of each A, B and C piece and position around marked circle, again using the full-size drawing as a guide for placement of pieces. Hand-stitch in place using matching all-purpose thread.

Step 7. Position and stitch the 3/8"-wide dark green bias tape in place around marked circle and on top of the ends of the A, B and C pieces.

Petals & Leaves Pillow
Placement Diagram
17" x 17"

Step 8. To make a flower petal, place two D pieces right sides together; stitch around curved edges. Clip curves and turn right side out; press. Repeat for 20 petals.

Step 9. To make one flower, using a needle with knotted thread, gather five petals together on the thread; pull thread tight and place in a circle on the bias tape referring to Figure 3, using the full-size pattern drawing as a guide for placement on the bias tape. Hand-stitch in place using the same thread as gathering stitches to secure centers of petals to the background. Repeat for four flower motifs.

Step 10. Sew a 3/4" gold button in the center of each flower motif to cover raw edges and stitches.

Figure 3
Gather 5 petals together on the
thread; pull thread tight and
place in a circle on the bias tape.

Step 11. Sandwich batting between the completed pillow top and the prepared backing square; pin or baste layers together to hold flat.

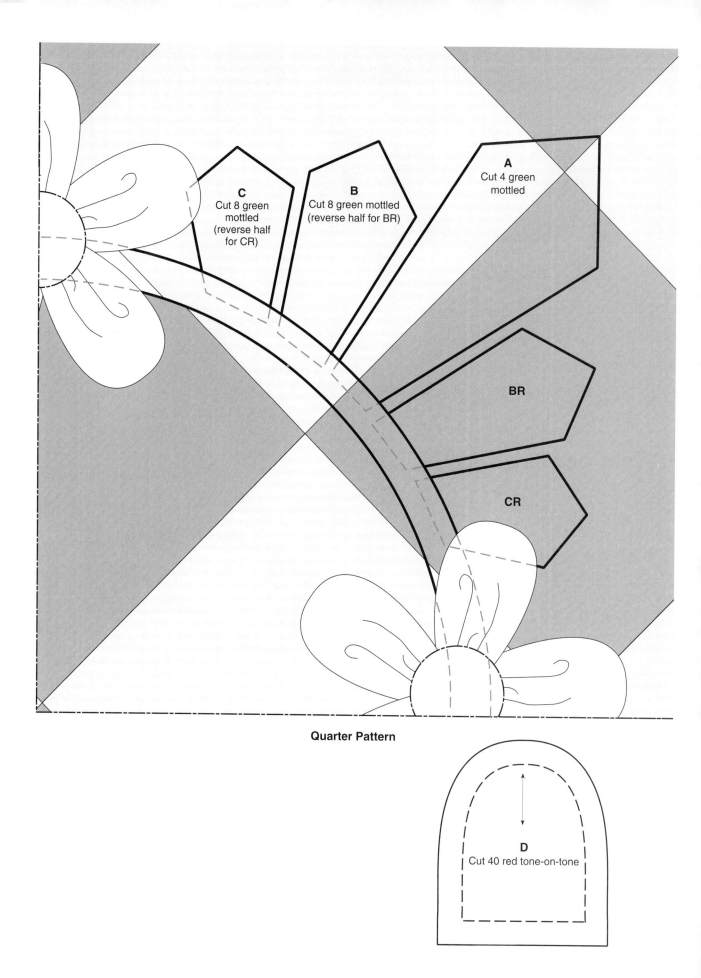

Quarter Pattern

C
Cut 8 green mottled (reverse half for CR)

B
Cut 8 green mottled (reverse half for BR)

A
Cut 4 green mottled

BR

CR

D
Cut 40 red tone-on-tone

Step 12. Quilt as desired by hand or machine. *Note: The pillow shown was hand-quilted in the ditch of background seams and around outer edge bias tape using cream hand-quilting thread.*

Step 13. When quilting is complete, remove pins or basting and trim excess batting and backing even with pillow-top edges.

Step 14. Cover the 1 1/4" button with green mottled as directed with button. Sew to the center of the quilted pillow-top.

Step 15. Using a zipper foot, machine-baste the 3/8"-wide red cord with lip to the edges of the quilted pillow top, overlapping beginning and end as shown in Figure 4.

Step 16. Cut a 17 1/2" x 17 1/2" square red/green/white plaid for pillow back.

Figure 4
Overlap beginning and end of cord as shown.

Step 17. Place the pillow back right sides together with the quilted/corded pillow front. Using the zipper foot, machine-stitch all around, leaving a 10" opening on one side.

Step 18. Turn right side out; poke out corners. Stuff with polyester fiberfill to desired fullness.

Step 19. Hand-stitch the opening closed to finish. ❖

Flowers & Grapes Baskets
Continued from page 122

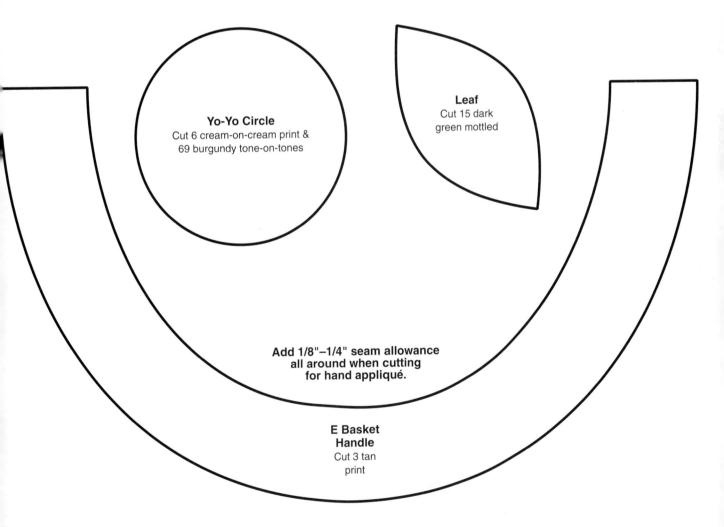

Yo-Yo Circle
Cut 6 cream-on-cream print &
69 burgundy tone-on-tones

Leaf
Cut 15 dark
green mottled

**Add 1/8"–1/4" seam allowance
all around when cutting
for hand appliqué.**

**E Basket
Handle**
Cut 3 tan
print

JOHN JAMES

Betweens
Mi-Longues
Nähnadeln
halblang

Article No
L4311

Size
No

silk - finish

3 150m 164 yds

Appliqué for Fun

Pumpkins, baskets, flowers and butterflies decorate these quilts and projects stitched from fat quarters, created to give your home a warm, friendly look.

Spring Bouquets

By Marian Shenk

*Spring flowers bring joy whether they are plants,
cut flowers in a vase or fabric flowers on a wall quilt.*

Project Specifications

Skill Level: Intermediate

Quilt Size: 44" x 45"

Materials

- 1 fat quarter gray mottled
- 1 fat quarter each 2 different mauve prints
- 1 fat quarter each 2 different rose prints
- 1 fat quarter each 2 different burgundy prints
- 1 fat quarter each 3 different green prints ranging from light to dark
- 1/2 yard burgundy print for binding
- 1 1/4 yards cream-on-cream print for background
- 1 1/2 yards burgundy border stripe for sashing and outside borders
- Batting 48" x 49"
- Backing 48" x 49"
- All-purpose thread to match fabrics
- Cream hand-quilting thread
- 2 packages dark green narrow bias tape for stems
- 1 yard 3/8"-wide mauve ribbon
- 1/4 yard 1/2"-wide burgundy ribbon
- 15 (1/2") burgundy buttons
- 25 (1/2") rose buttons
- Basic sewing tools and supplies, rotary cutter, mat and ruler and water-erasable marker or pencil

Instructions

Step 1. Cut the following from cream-on-cream print for appliqué background pieces: 25 1/2" x 10 1/2" for A; 13 1/2" x 13 1/2" for B; 13 1/2" x 10 1/2" for C; 13 1/2" x 13 1/2" for D; 12 1/2" x 12 1/2" for E; 12 1/2" x 14 1/2" for F; 12 1/2" x 16 1/2" for G; and 12 1/2" x 10 1/2" for H. Fold each piece in quarters and press to form creases to mark centers.

Step 2. Cut the following dark green narrow bias tape for stems: eight 1 1/4", two 8 3/4" and one 2 3/4" for A; one each 5 1/2", 6", 6 1/2" and 8 1/4" for B; two 1 1/4", two 7 1/2" and one 4 1/4" for C; four 4 3/4" for D; two 3" and one 2" for E; two 3 1/2", two 2 3/4"

Spring Bouquets
Placement Diagram
44" x 45"

and one 3 1/4" for F; one 2 1/4", one 3 3/4", one 5 1/4", two 7" and one 7 1/2" for G; and one 2 1/4" and two 5 1/2" for H.

Step 3. Cut and prepare appliqué pieces for hand appliqué referring to the General Instructions. Cut a 4 1/8" piece 3/8"-wide mauve ribbon; hand-stitch on vase F piece referring to pattern for positioning.

Step 4. Referring to Figure 1, arrange stem pieces on each background piece; pin in place. Arrange remaining pieces in numerical order as shown in Figure 2; hand-stitch in place using matching all-purpose thread.

Step 5. Choose a stripe from the length of the burgundy border stripe fabric; cut two 1 1/2" x 13 1/2" J strips, two 1 1/2" x 12 1/2" K strips, one 1 1/2" x 27 1/2" L strip, one 1 1/2"x 25 1/2" M strip and one 1 1/2" x 38 1/2" N strip from chosen stripe section.

Step 6. Join B, C and D with two J strips to make a row as shown in Figure 3; press seams toward J strips.

Step 7. Join E and F with one K strip as shown in Figure 4; press seams toward K.

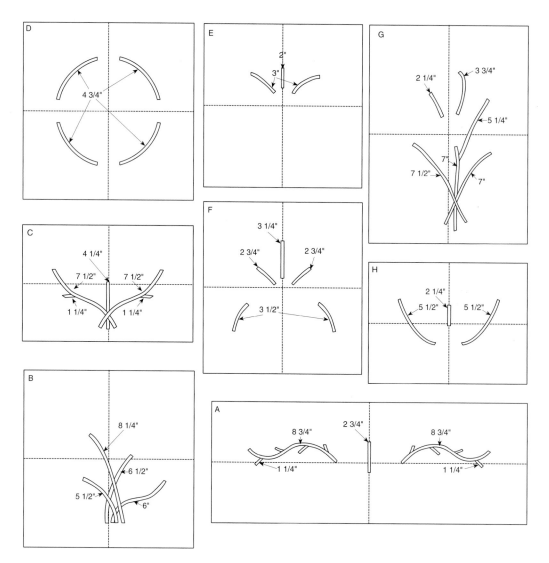

Figure 1
Arrange stem pieces on background pieces using creased centerlines on background pieces as guides for placement as shown.

Figure 2
Arrange appliqué shapes on background pieces as shown.

Figure 2
Arrange appliqué shapes on background pieces as shown.

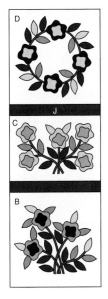

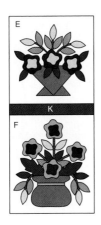

Figure 3
Join B, C and D with 2 J
strips to make a row.

Figure 4
Join E and F
with 1 K strip.

Step 8. Join G and H with one K strip as shown in Figure 5; press seams toward K.

Step 9. Join the G-K-H row and the E-K-F row with L as shown in Figure 6; press seams toward L.

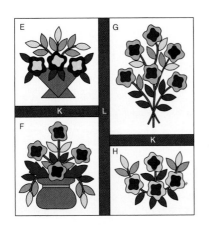

Figure 5
Join G and H
with 1 K strip.

Figure 6
Join the G-K-H row and the
E-K-F row with L.

Step 10. Join the pieced section and A with M as shown in Figure 7; press seams toward M.

Step 11. Join the two pieced sections with N to complete the pieced center as shown in Figure 8; press seams toward N.

Step 12. Choose another stripe section from the burgundy border stripe fabric; cut four 3 1/2" x 48" identical strips from the chosen section for O strips.

Step 13. Sew an O strip to each side of the pieced center section, mitering corners. Trim excess at corners; press mitered seam open.

Step 14. Cut one 8" piece each 1/2"-wide burgundy

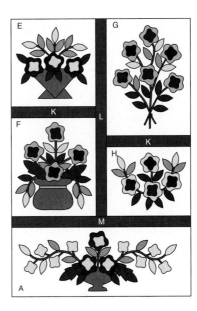

Figure 7
Join the pieced section and A with M.

Figure 8
Join the 2 pieced sections with N to complete the pieced center.

and 3/8"-wide mauve ribbon. Place together; tie knot in center. Hand-stitch on stems on G; trim ribbon ends.

Step 15. Cut a 10" piece 3/8"-wide mauve ribbon; hand-stitch center on ribbon strip on vase F piece; tie in bow and trim ends.

Step 16. Sew a rose or burgundy button in the center of each flower referring to the Placement Diagram for positioning and color placement.

Step 17. Prepare for quilting and quilt as desired referring to the General Instructions. ***Note:** The project shown was hand-quilted around appliqué shapes using cream hand-quilting thread.*

Step 18. Prepare 5 1/2 yards burgundy print binding and apply referring to the General Instructions to finish. ❖

Flower Center
Cut 5 mauve, 17
burgundy & 18
rose prints

Large Leaf
Cut 4 dark green print

Vase E
Cut 1 gray mottled

Small Leaf
Cut 26 light,
41 medium
& 44 dark
green prints

Flower
Cut 9 rose, 10 burgundy
& 13 mauve prints

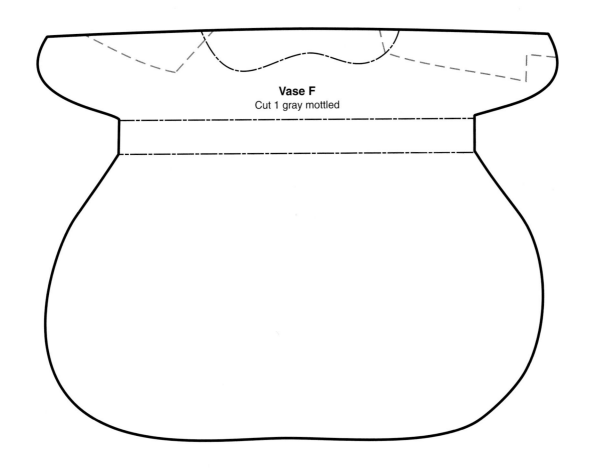

Vase F
Cut 1 gray mottled

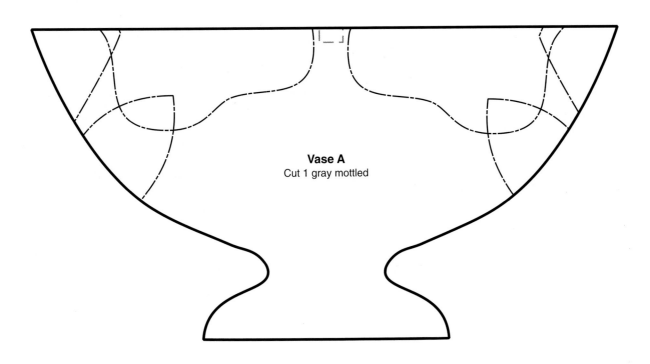

Vase A
Cut 1 gray mottled

Oriental Garden

By Christine Schultz

An Oriental print creates the unusual borders on this little wall quilt.

Project Specifications

Skill Level: Intermediate

Quilt Size: 20 1/2" x 20 1/2"

Materials

- 1 fat quarter red solid
- 1 fat quarter each green and brown mottleds
- 5/8 yard white-on-white print
- 3/4 yard Oriental print
- Batting 25" x 25"
- Backing 25" x 25"
- All-purpose thread to match fabrics
- White hand-quilting thread
- Green 6-strand embroidery floss
- Heat-resistant template plastic
- Spray starch
- Basic sewing supplies and tools, large plain paper, freezer paper, tweezers and water-erasable marker or pencil

Instructions

Step 1. Prewash and press all fabrics.

Step 2. Cut a 21" x 21" square each plain paper and white-on-white print. Fold each square in fourths to find the center; crease.

Step 3. Transfer the one-quarter appliqué pattern given to each quarter of the paper square.

Step 4. Place the fabric square on the marked paper pattern matching crease lines. Using the water-erasable marker or pencil, transfer the design onto the fabric square.

Step 5. Cut a 10" x 10" square freezer paper; fold in eighths as shown in Figure 1.

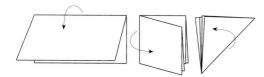

Figure 1
Cut a 10" x 10" square freezer
paper; fold in eighths.

Step 6. Open paper and align folds with green-shaded butterfly section of the appliqué design. Trace the partial butterfly design on the paper as shown in Figure 2. Refold paper and staple in blank areas around the design so paper doesn't shift while cutting. Cut butterfly on drawn lines.

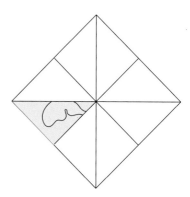

Figure 2
Trace the partial butterfly design
highlighted in green on the pattern
onto 1/8 of the paper.

Step 7. Open cut paper and lay shiny side down on wrong side of brown mottled; press with a hot, dry iron to temporarily fuse paper to fabric. Using sharp scissors, cut around paper leaving a 3/16" turn-under seam allowance around inside and outside edges. Carefully clip curves and angles.

Step 8. Pin design, paper side down to the background square, using marked lines on square as placement guides. Hand-stitch butterfly shape in place using matching all-purpose thread, turning under seam allowance as you stitch.

Step 9. Carefully slash the background fabric behind the butterfly shape and pull freezer paper away from inside using tweezers.

Step 10. Trace leaf shapes on the dull side of the freezer paper. Lay shiny side down on the wrong side

of green mottled; press with a hot, dry iron to temporarily fuse paper to fabric. Cut out, leaving a 3/16" turn-under seam allowance. Clip curves and angles.

Step 11. Pin leaves in place on the background square using marked lines as placement guides. Hand-stitch in place using matching all-purpose thread, turning under seam allowance as you stitch.

Step 12. Remove freezer paper as in Step 9.

Step 13. Using 2 strands green embroidery floss, stem-stitch along marked stem lines.

Step 14. Trace and cut a template from the heat-resistant template material for the cherry shape using the pattern given.

Step 15. Cut 64 red solid circle shapes using the 1" circle pattern given.

Step 16. Baste around edge of each circle shape with a knotted thread, leaving a 3" tail as shown in Figure 3.

Figure 3
Baste around edge of each
circle shape with a knotted
thread, leaving a 3" tail.

Step 17. To make a perfect circle cherry, spray red fabric circle with spray starch to saturate. Place cherry template in center of circle on wrong side and draw up threads tightly so fabric hugs the template and all raw edges are gathered in the center; press firmly with iron on both sides.

Step 18. Cut thread tails closely; using tweezers, gently open the gathers just enough to pull out the template; finger-press circle back in shape.

Step 19. Using red all-purpose thread, stitch cherries in place on stems along marked lines.

Step 20. Cut a 25"-long piece freezer paper (along length of roll). Fold in half along length; trace border design onto freezer paper four times, with fold line on pattern placed on paper fold as shown in Figure 4.

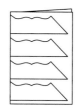

Figure 4
Trace border design onto
freezer paper 4 times.

Step 21. Cut out four freezer-paper border pieces and iron on the wrong side of the Oriental print. Cut out fabric shapes, adding a 1/4" seam allowance all around when cutting.

Step 22. Stitch border pieces together at corner diagonal seam to form the frame. *Note: Handle pieces gently so paper doesn't come away from fabric before the appliqué is complete; re-press, if necessary.*

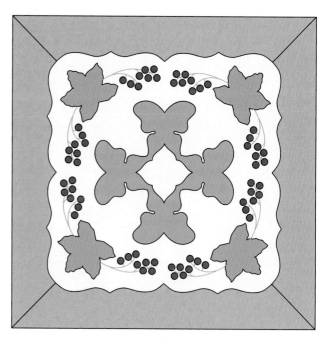

Oriental Garden
Placement Diagram
20 1/2" x 20 1/2"

Step 23. Lay the border section over the appliquéd background square, aligning outside edges and inside edges referring to marked lines. Hand-stitch in place using matching all-purpose thread, turning under seam allowance as you stitch.

Step 24. Remove paper and trim background fabric seam allowance under border to 1/4".

Step 25. Remove all markings from background as directed with marker instructions.

Step 26. Press completed top.

Step 27. Prepare quilt top for quilting and finish referring to the General Instructions. *Note: The quilt shown was hand-quilted in a diagonal grid, on leaf stem lines and around each appliquéd piece using white hand-quilting thread.*

Step 28. Prepare 2 3/4 yards Oriental print binding and apply referring to the General Instructions to finish. ❖

1" Circle

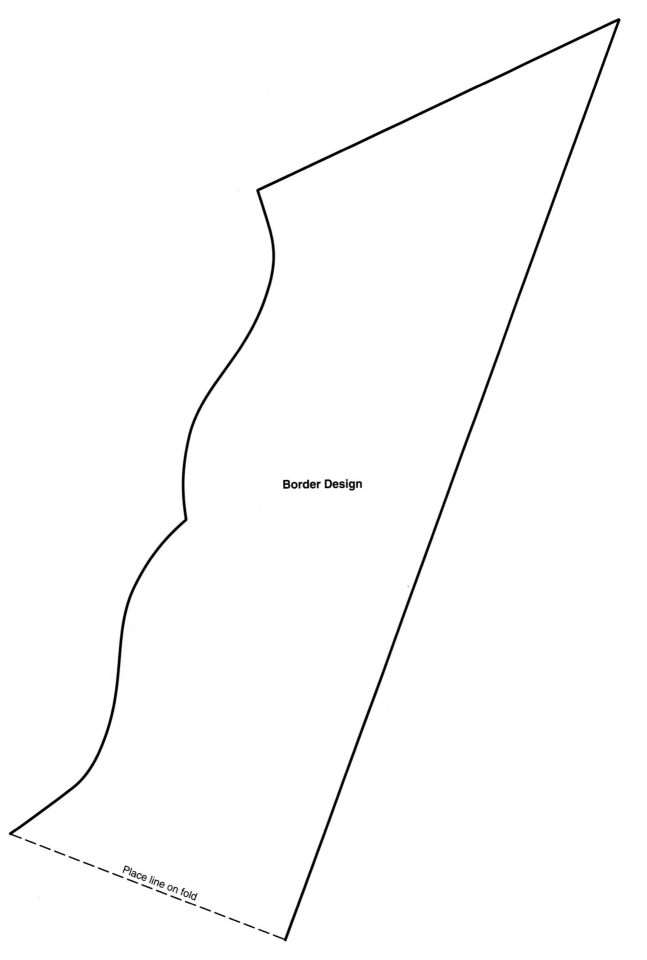

Border Design

Place line on fold

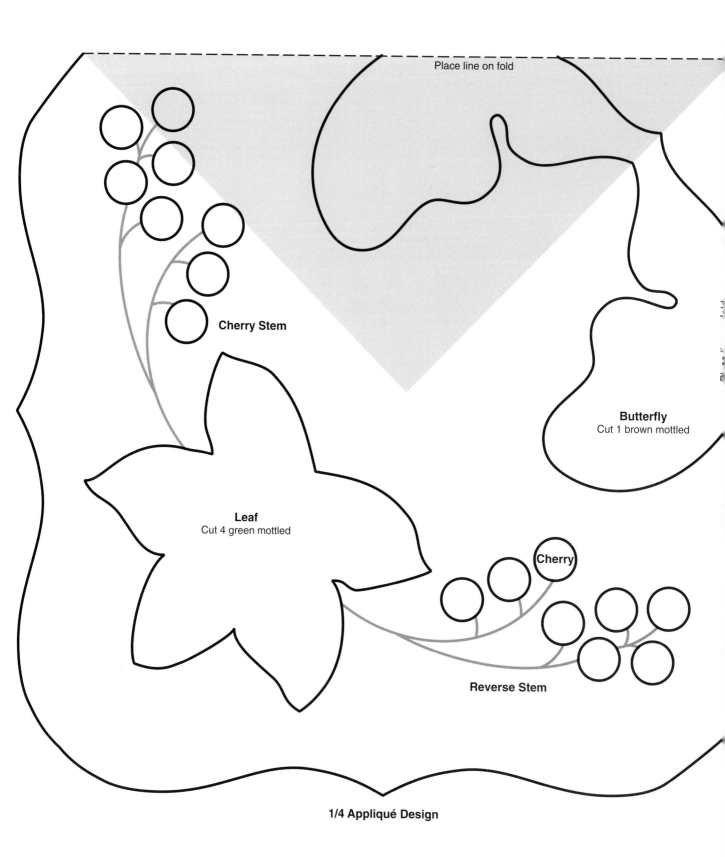

Place line on fold

Cherry Stem

Butterfly
Cut 1 brown mottled

Leaf
Cut 4 green mottled

Cherry

Reverse Stem

1/4 Appliqué Design

Flower Basket Mantel Cover

By Kate Laucomer

Make a pieced-and-appliquéd mantel cover to decorate your fireplace mantel for summer.

Project Notes

The mantel cover size given may not fit your mantel. It may be adjusted in length in increments of 9 1/4" and can be made any depth by changing the size of the depth piece.

Begin by measuring the length of your mantel. Divide this number by 9 1/4 (the size of the diagonal of the block) and round to the nearest whole number. For example a 65" mantel divided by 9 1/4 equals 7.02; round off to 7. This mantel cover would require seven blocks.

To determine the depth of the mantel cover piece, measure the depth of the mantel from front to back; add 1/2" for seam allowance. If your mantel depth is 10", you would cut your fabric pieces 10 1/2" wide.

The instructions are given for a mantel cover that finishes at 64 3/4" x 9 1/4" x 9 1/4".

Project Specifications

Skill Level: Intermediate

Mantel Cover Size: 64 3/4" x 9 1/4" x 9 1/4"

Block Size: 6 1/2" x 6 1/2"

Number of Blocks: 7

Basket
6 1/2" x 6 1/2" Block

Materials

- Scraps green prints and mottleds for leaves
- 1 fat quarter each purple, yellow, peach, green, pink, mauve and light blue mottleds or tone-on-tones
- 1 fat quarter each blue print and blue stripe
- 2 fat quarters cream print
- Batting 65" x 20"
- Backing 65" x 20"
- All-purpose thread to match fabrics
- Cream and green machine-quilting thread
- 3/4 yard lightweight fusible transfer web
- 3/4 yard fabric stabilizer
- Basic sewing tools and supplies, rotary cutter, mat and ruler

Instructions

Step 1. Cut seven squares cream print 7" x 7" for background. Fold and crease each square to mark centers.

Step 2. Trace the basket, flower and leaf shapes onto the paper side of the lightweight fusible transfer web as directed on the pattern for number to cut.

Step 3. Cut out shapes, leaving a margin around each one. Fuse each shape to the wrong side of fabrics as directed on each piece for color; cut out shapes on traced line. Remove paper backing.

Step 4. Center a basket motif on the diagonal crease line of one background square; fuse in place. Arrange and fuse remaining pieces on top of basket shape in numerical order referring to the pattern. Repeat for seven blocks.

Step 5. Cut a piece of fabric stabilizer to fit behind each fused square; pin in place.

Step 6. Using all-purpose thread to match fabrics, stitch a machine buttonhole stitch around each shape.

Step 7. When stitching is complete, remove fabric stabilizer.

Step 8. Draw three 7 3/8" x 7 3/8" squares and one 7 3/4" x 7 3/4" square on paper; cut the 7 3/4" paper square in half on both diagonals; discard two paper triangles.

Step 9. Cut two or three 1 1/4" x 22" strips from each mottled or tone-or-tone fat quarter and eight 1 1/4" x 22" strips cream print.

Step 10. Center a colored fabric strip on one square; pin in place. Sew a cream print strip on each side; press flat and trim, leaving excess on each end as shown in Figure 1.

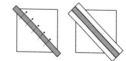

Figure 1
Sew a cream print strip on each side; press flat and trim, leaving excess on each end.

Step 11. Continue to add strips alternating colored and cream print strips to cover the paper as shown in Figure 2; repeat for three covered paper squares.

Repeat to cover the two paper triangles as shown in Figure 3.

Figure 2
Continue to add strips alternating colored and cream print strips to cover the paper.

Figure 3
Cover 2 paper triangles as shown.

Step 12. Trim fabric pieces even with edges of the paper as shown in Figure 4. Cut the squares in half on one diagonal to make triangles as shown in Figure 5.

Figure 4
Trim fabric pieces even with edges of the paper.

Figure 5
Cut the squares in half on 1 diagonal to make triangles.

Step 13. Sew a large triangle to the top left edge of six Basket blocks as shown in Figure 6; press seams toward Basket block.

Figure 6
Sew a large triangle
to the top left edge of
6 Basket blocks.

Step 14. Join the pieced units and add the triangles to the ends as shown in Figure 7; press seams toward pieced units.

Figure 7
Join the pieced units and add
the triangles to the ends.

Step 15. Cut one 9 3/4" x 9 3/4" square from each mottled or tone-on-tone fat quarter. Join to make a long strip; press seams in one direction.

Step 16. Sew the pieced strip to the pieced basket unit as shown in Figure 8; press seams toward the pieced strip. Remove paper from the strip-pieced triangles.

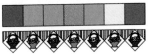

Figure 8
Sew the pieced strip to
the pieced basket unit.

Step 17. Lay the batting and backing pieces on a flat surface. Place the pieced top right sides together with the backing piece; trim batting and backing using the pieced top as the pattern.

Step 18. Lay the batting piece on a flat surface; place the pieced top on the batting and the backing piece right sides together with the pieced top.

Step 19. Stitch all around outside edge, leaving an 8" opening on the long straight side; trim points and clip corners. Turn right side out through opening. Poke out points and press; hand-stitch opening closed.

Step 20. Quilt as desired by hand or machine. ***Note:** The sample shown was machine-quilted in the cream-on-cream background areas 1/8" from appliqué motifs using cream machine-quilting thread and in a feather design on the pieced strip using green machine-quilting thread. Topstitch 1/8" from outside edges to finish.* ❖

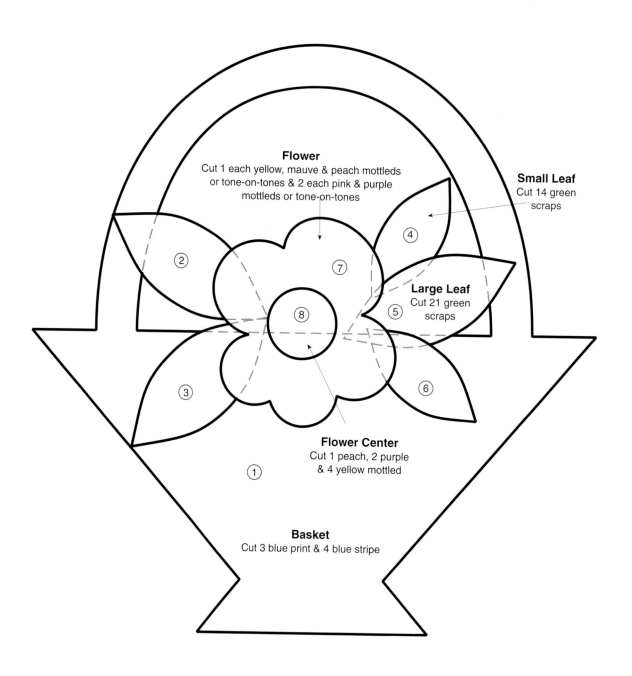

Flower
Cut 1 each yellow, mauve & peach mottleds
or tone-on-tones & 2 each pink & purple
mottleds or tone-on-tones

Small Leaf
Cut 14 green
scraps

Large Leaf
Cut 21 green
scraps

Flower Center
Cut 1 peach, 2 purple
& 4 yellow mottled

Basket
Cut 3 blue print & 4 blue stripe

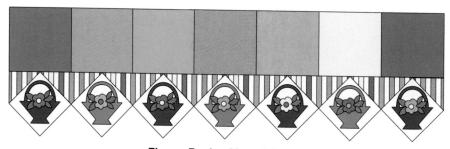

Flower Basket Mantel Cover
Placement Diagram
64 3/4" x 9 1/4" x 9 1/4"

Homespun Pumpkin Patch Vest

By Julie Weaver

Make a quilted flannel vest for those cool autumn days.

Project Specifications

Skill Level: Beginner

Vest Size: Size Varies

Materials

- Commercial vest pattern
- Fabric for vest back and lining as listed on commercial pattern
- Flannel scraps in green, rust and brown
- 4 different navy flannel fat quarters
- 1 yard muslin
- 1 yard thin batting
- Neutral color all-purpose thread
- Dark blue machine-quilting thread
- Brown 6-strand embroidery floss
- 1/2 yard fusible transfer web
- Basic sewing supplies and tools

Homespun Pumpkin Patch Vest
Placement Diagram
Size Varies

Instructions

Step 1. Cut two pieces muslin several inches larger all around than the commercial vest front pattern piece.

Step 2. Piece flannel fat quarters onto each muslin foundation referring to Figure 1 using two fat quarters for the left front and two fat quarters for the right front. *Note: Figure 1 is a guide for piecing the fronts; you may piece them any way you desire.*

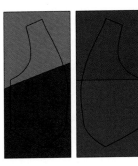

Figure 1
Piece fat quarters for each
front piece as shown.

Step 3. Layer each pieced section with a same-size batting piece. Quilt each piece in a meandering design using dark blue machine-quilting thread.

Step 4. When quilting is complete, cut out vest front pieces using commerical pattern.

Step 5. Trace appliqué shapes onto the paper side of the fusible transfer web as directed on each piece for number to cut. Cut out shapes, leaving a margin around each one.

Step 6. Fuse paper shapes to the wrong side of the flannel scraps as directed on each piece for color. Cut out shapes on traced lines; remove paper backing.

Step 7. Arrange the appliqué shapes on the vest right front in numerical order referring to the Placement Diagram for positioning and the pattern for order; when satisfied with positioning, fuse shapes in place.

Step 8. Using 3 strands of brown embroidery floss, blanket-stitch around each pumpkin, leaf and stem shape. Chain-stitch pumpkin ribs, leaf veins and vines referring to patterns for placement and Figure 2 for stitches.

Step 9. Finish vest referring to commerical pattern instructions. ❖

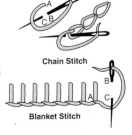

Chain Stitch

Blanket Stitch

Figure 2
Chain-stitch detail lines;
blanket-stitch around
outside edges of pieces.

Appliqué for Fun **159**

Leaf
Cut 5 green
flannel scraps

Stem
Cut 3 brown flannel scraps
(reverse 1)

③

②

④

①

Large Pumpkin
Cut 1 rust flannel scrap

⑥

⑦

⑪

⑨

⑩

⑤

Medium Pumpkin
Cut 1 rust flannel scrap

⑧

Small Pumpkin
Cut 1 rust flannel scrap

Posy Silhouettes

By Leslie Beck

*Pieced spool blocks are the vases for the stitched
and appliquéd flowers in this simple quilted banner.*

Project Specifications

Skill Level: Beginner

Quilt Size: 24" x 15 1/2"

Block Size: 4" x 4"

Number of Blocks: 4

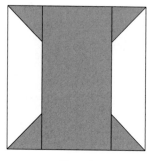

Spool
4" x 4" Block

Materials

- Scraps of green and rose prints, solids or mottleds
- 1 fat quarter each rose, navy, green and purple tone-on-tones
- 1 fat quarter cream-on-cream print
- 1/4 yard blue tone-on-tone for border
- 1/4 yard dark rose print for binding
- Batting 28" x 20"
- Backing 28" x 20"
- All-purpose thread to match fabrics
- Cream machine-quilting thread
- Green, purple, blue and pink 6-strand embroidery floss
- 1/4 yard lightweight fusible transfer web
- 4 (1/2") colored buttons
- Basic sewing tools and supplies, rotary cutter, mat and ruler and water-erasable marker or pencil

Instructions

Step 1. Trace flower motif pieces onto the paper side of the lightweight fusible transfer web as directed on the pattern for number to cut.

Step 2. Cut out shapes, leaving a margin around each one. Fuse each shape to the wrong side of fabrics as directed on each piece for color; cut out shapes on traced line. Remove paper backing.

Step 3. Cut a 7" x 19 1/2" rectangle cream-on-cream print for background.

Step 4. Measure in 6 3/4" from the left side edge and mark as shown in Figure 1.

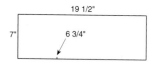

Figure 1
Measure in 6 3/4" from the
left side edge and mark.

Step 5. Position the flower motif stem at the mark; slip leaf shapes under stem referring to the pattern for placement; fuse in place. Arrange and fuse remaining pieces in numerical order referring to the pattern; set aside.

Step 6. To piece the Spool blocks, cut one 2 1/2" x 4 1/2" rectangle from each tone-on-tone fat quarter for A.

Step 7. Cut eleven 1 1/2" x 4 1/2" rectangles cream-on-cream print for B; set aside three B pieces for sashing strips.

Step 8. Cut four 1 1/2" x 1 1/2" squares from each tone-on-tone fat quarter for C. Mark a diagonal line from corner to corner on the wrong side of each C square.

Step 9. Place a C square right sides together with B as shown in Figure 2; stitch on marked line. Trim excess seam to 1/4"; press C to the right side.

Figure 2
Place a C square right
sides together with B.

Step 10. Repeat with a matching fabric C on the opposite end of B to complete a B-C unit as shown in Figure 3; repeat for eight B-C units.

Step 11. Sew a B-C unit to opposite long sides of A, matching C color with A as shown in Figure 4 to complete one Spool block; repeat for four blocks.

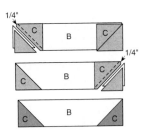

Figure 3
Complete the B-C unit as shown.

Figure 4
Sew a B-C unit to opposite long sides of A, matching C color with A to complete 1 Spool block.

Step 12. Trace four star shapes onto the paper side of the lightweight fusible transfer web; cut out shapes leaving a margin around each one. Fuse to fabrics as directed on piece. Cut out fused star shapes on traced lines; remove paper backing.

Step 13. Fuse a star shape to the center of each A piece on each Spool block referring to the Placement Diagram for color placement.

Step 14. Machine buttonhole-stitch around each star shape using all-purpose thread to match fabrics; repeat with fused flower shapes.

Step 15. Join the blocks with the remaining B pieces as shown in Figure 5 to complete the pieced section.

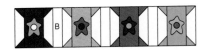

Figure 5
Join the blocks with the remaining B pieces to complete the pieced section.

Step 16. Sew the appliquéd section to the pieced section to complete the center; press seam away from pieced section.

Step 17. Mark the stitching motif pattern given in the empty background above the three Spool blocks referring to the Placement Diagram for positioning.

Step 18. Using 2 strands green embroidery floss, backstitch along marked lines for leaves and stems. Repeat with blue, pink and purple embroidery floss for flowers referring to the Placement Diagram for color placement.

Step 19. Make French knots in the flower centers as shown in Figure 6 using embroidery floss to match flower tops.

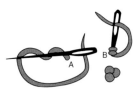

Figure 6
Make French knots in
the flower centers.

Step 20. Cut two strips each 1" x 11" and 1" x 20 1/2" rose tone-on-tone. Sew the shorter strips to opposite short sides and the longer strips to opposite long sides; press seams toward strips.

Step 21. Cut two strips each 2 1/2" x 12" and 2 1/2" x 24 1/2" blue tone-on-tone. Sew the shorter strips to opposite short sides and the longer strips to opposite long sides; press seams toward strips.

Step 22. Prepare for quilting and quilt as desired referring to the General Instructions. *Note: The sample shown was machine-quilted in the cream-on-cream background areas with a meandering design using cream machine-quilting thread. The borders were stitched in the ditch using all-purpose thread to match fabrics.*

Step 23. Prepare 2 3/4 yards self-made dark rose print binding and apply referring to the General Instructions.

Step 24. Sew a button in the center of each star to finish. ❖

Posy Silhouettes
Placement Diagram
24" x 15 1/2"

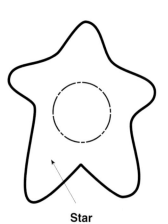

Star
Cut 1 each rose, green, navy
& purple tone-on-tone

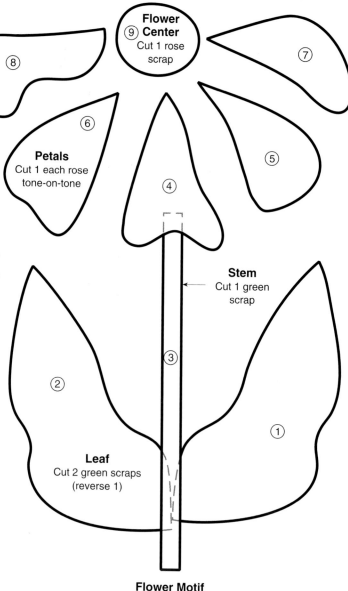

Flower Motif

Pattern continued on page 169

Flowers at the Crossroads

By Marian Shenk

Appliquéd flower blocks combine with pieced blocks in this pretty wall quilt.

Project Specifications

Skill Level: Intermediate

Quilt Size: 27 1/2" x 27 1/2"

Block Size: 7 1/2" x 7 1/2"

Number of Blocks: 9

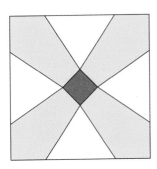

Crossroads
7 1/2" x 7 1/2" Block

Corner Flower
7 1/2" x 7 1/2" Block

Materials

- 1 fat quarter each light and dark green prints
- 1 fat quarter each yellow and gold prints
- 1 fat quarter burgundy print
- 1 fat quarter mauve mottled
- 2 fat quarters cream-on-cream print
- 1/4 yard green-on-green print
- All-purpose thread to match fabrics
- Cream hand-quilting thread
- 1 package green solid narrow bias tape for stems
- 1 package green solid wide bias tape for binding
- Basic sewing supplies and tools and water-erasable marker or pencil

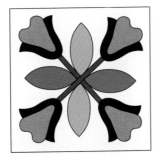

Center Flower
7 1/2" x 7 1/2" Block

Instructions

Crossroads Blocks

Step 1. Prepare templates using pattern pieces given; cut as directed on each piece.

Step 2. Sew C to opposite long sides of B as shown in Figure 1; repeat for two B-C units. Press seams toward C.

Figure 1
Sew C to opposite
long sides of B.

Step 3. Sew B to opposite sides of A as shown in Figure 2; press seams toward B.

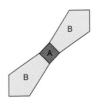

Figure 2
Sew B to opposite
sides of A.

Step 4. Sew a C-B unit to opposite sides of the A-B unit to complete one Crossroads block as shown in Figure 3; repeat for four blocks. Press seams toward C-B units.

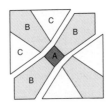

Figure 3
Sew a C-B unit to
opposite sides of the A-B
unit to complete 1 block.

Corner Flower Blocks

Step 1. Prepare templates for appliqué pieces; cut and prepare for hand appliqué, adding a 1/4" seam allowance all around when cutting.

Step 2. Cut five 8" x 8" squares cream-on-cream print for background; fold and crease to mark diagonal centers. Set aside one square for Center Flower block.

Step 3. Arrange two dark green print and two light green print leaves and three flower motifs with one long stem and one base stem piece using crease lines as a guide and referring to Figure 4 for placement; pin or baste in place.

Figure 4
Arrange pieces on
background block as shown.

Step 4. Appliqué shapes in place by hand using all-purpose thread to match fabrics. Repeat for four Corner Flower blocks.

Center Flower Block

Step 1. Using previously cut fabric patches and creased background square, arrange two center stems with dark green print and two light green print leaves and four flower motifs using crease lines as a guide and referring to Figure 5 for placement; pin or baste in place.

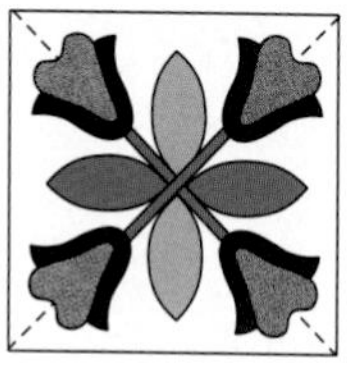

Figure 5
Arrange pieces on
background block as shown.

Step 2. Appliqué shapes in place by hand using all-purpose thread to match fabrics to complete the Center Flower block.

Finishing

Step 1. Join two Corner Flower blocks with one Crossroads block to make a row referring to Figure 6; press seams away from appliquéd blocks. Repeat for two rows.

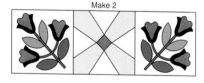

Make 2

Figure 6
Join blocks to make a row as shown.

Step 2. Join two Crossroads blocks with one Center Flower block to make the center row referring to Figure 7; press seams away from appliquéd block.

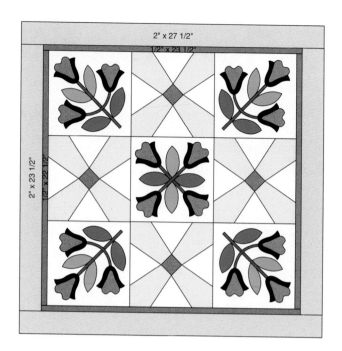

2" x 27 1/2"
1/2" x 23 1/2"
2" x 23 1/2"
1/2" x 23 1/2"

Flowers at the Crossroads
Placement Diagram
27 1/2" x 27 1/2"

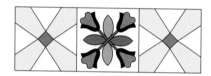

Figure 7
Join blocks to make a row as shown.

Step 3. Join the rows referring to the Placement Diagram for positioning of rows; press seams in one direction.

Step 4. Cut and piece two strips each 1" x 23" and 1" x 24" from gold print fat quarter. Sew the shorter strips to opposite sides and longer strips to the remaining sides of the pieced top; press seams toward strips.

Step 5. Cut two strips each 2 1/2" x 24" and 2 1/2" x 28" green-on-green print. Sew the shorter strips to opposite sides and longer strips to remaining sides of the pieced top; press seams toward strips.

Step 6. Prepare quilt top for quilting and finish referring to the General Instructions. *Note: The sample was hand-quilted in the ditch of seams on pieced blocks with cream hand-quilting thread. The appliquéd shapes were outline-quilted using cream hand-quilting thread. A cable design was hand-quilted in the outside border strips using cream hand-quilting thread.*

Step 7. When quilting is complete, prepare for binding and bind edges with green solid wide bias tape referring to the General Instructions to finish. ❖

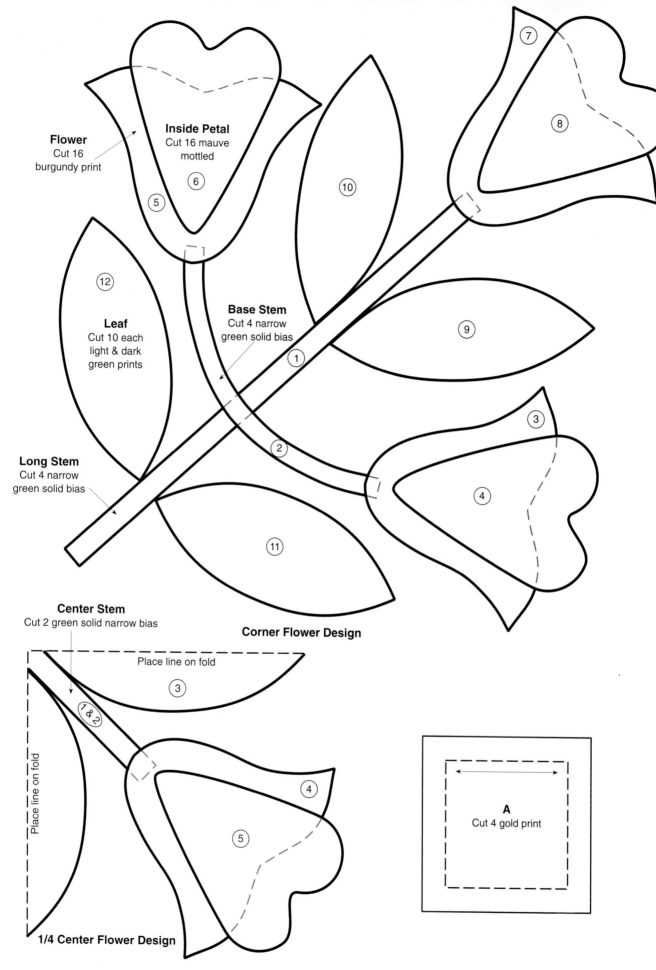

Flower
Cut 16
burgundy print

Inside Petal
Cut 16 mauve
mottled

⑥

⑤

⑦

⑧

⑩

Leaf
Cut 10 each
light & dark
green prints

⑫

Base Stem
Cut 4 narrow
green solid bias

①

⑨

②

③

④

Long Stem
Cut 4 narrow
green solid bias

⑪

Corner Flower Design

Center Stem
Cut 2 green solid narrow bias

Place line on fold

③

1 & 2

Place line on fold

④

⑤

A
Cut 4 gold print

1/4 Center Flower Design

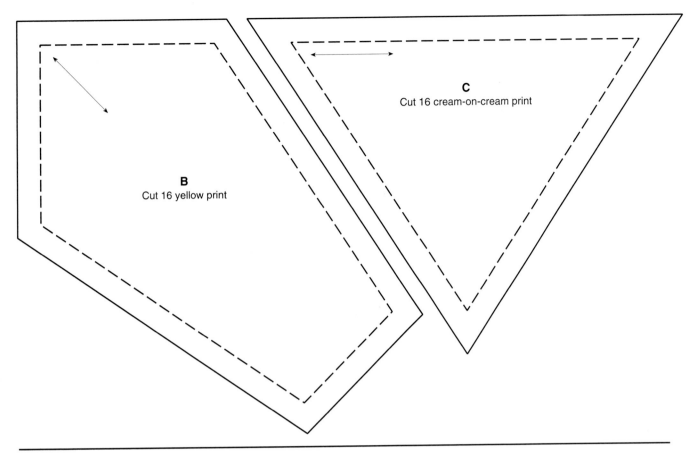

B
Cut 16 yellow print

C
Cut 16 cream-on-cream print

Posey Silhouettes

Continued from page 164

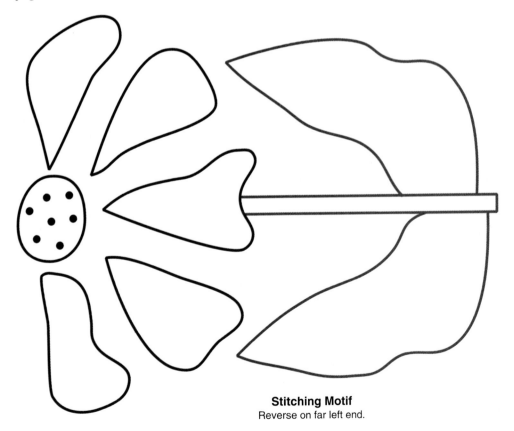

Stitching Motif
Reverse on far left end.

General Instructions

Fat-Quarter Fabrics

Fat quarters are fabric yardage that is cut half the fabric width by half a yard—in most fabrics this size would be 22" x 18". For some projects, this size works better than a regular quarter-yard of fabric that would be 9" by the width of the fabric, usually 42"–45".

Some projects require pieces larger than 9" for appliqué shapes or corner triangles. These larger shapes cannot be cut from a quarter-yard of fabric but can be cut from fat quarters.

Most fabric stores will not custom-cut fat quarters, but they do sell them. They choose which fabrics they want to cut up for this purpose. In some stores, just one fat quarter is available, while in other stores coordinated sets of fabric are selected and bundled in a attractive way to show off the colors. These bundles are hard to resist.

If you like to have lots of different fabrics available whenever you start to sew, collect fat quarters in a variety of colors and prints and get ready to have some fun.

We assume you have basic sewing and quilting skills and have all the tools and supplies needed to make quilts. We have included some basic instructions for quilting, making and adding binding and finishing your quilt.

Finishing Basics

Getting Ready to Quilt

Choosing a Quilting Design. If you choose to hand- or machine-quilt your finished top, you will need to choose a design for quilting.

There are several types of quilting designs, some of which may not have to be marked. The easiest of the unmarked designs is in-the-ditch quilting. Here the quilting stitches are placed in the valley created by the seams joining two pieces together or next to the edge of an appliqué design. There is no need to mark a top for in-the-ditch quilting. Machine quilters choose this option because the stitches are not as obvious on the finished quilt (Figure 1).

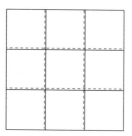

Figure 1
In-the-ditch quilting is done in the seam that joins 2 pieces.

Outline-quilting 1/4" or more away from seams or appliqué shapes is another no-mark alternative (Figure 2) which prevents having to sew through the layers made by seams, thus making stitching easier.

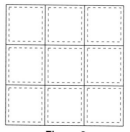

Figure 2
Outline-quilting 1/4" away from seam is a popular choice for quilting.

If you are not comfortable eyeballing the 1/4" (or other distance), masking tape is available in different widths and is helpful to place on straightedge designs to mark the quilting line. If using masking tape, place the tape right up against the seam and quilt close to the other edge.

Meander or free-motion quilting by machine fills in open spaces and doesn't require marking. It is fun and easy to stitch as shown in Figure 3.

Figure 3
Machine meander quilting fills in large spaces.

Marking the Top for Quilting or Tying. If you choose a fancy or allover design for quilting, you will need to transfer the design to your quilt top before layering with the backing and batting. You may use a sharp medium-lead or silver pencil on light background fabrics. Test the pencil marks to guarantee that they will wash out of your quilt top when quilting is complete; or be sure your quilting stitches cover the pencil marks. Mechanical pencils with very fine points may be used successfully to mark quilts.

Manufactured quilt-design templates are available in many designs and sizes and are cut out of a durable plastic template material that is easy to use.

To make a permanent quilt-design template, choose a template material on which to transfer the design. See-through plastic is the best choice as it will let you place the design while allowing you to see where it is in relation to your quilt design without moving it. Place the design on the quilt top where you want it and trace around it with your marking tool. Pick up the quilting template and place again; repeat marking.

No matter what marking method you use, remember, the marked lines should *never show* on the finished quilt. When the top is marked, it is ready for layering.

Preparing the Quilt Backing. The quilt backing is a very important feature of your quilt. In most cases, the materials list for each quilt in this book gives the size requirements for the backing, not the yardage needed. Exceptions to this are when the backing fabric is also used on the quilt top and yardage is given for that fabric.

A backing is generally cut at least 4" larger than the quilt top or 2" larger on all sides. For a 64" x 78" finished quilt, the backing would need to be at least 68" x 82".

To avoid having the seam across the center of the quilt backing, cut or tear one of the right-length pieces in half and sew half to each side of the second piece as shown in Figure 4.

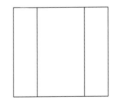

Figure 4
Center 1 backing piece with
a piece on each side.

Quilts that need a backing more than 88" wide may be pieced in horizontal pieces as shown in Figure 52.

Figure 5
Horizontal seams may be
used on backing pieces.

Layering the Quilt Sandwich. Layering the quilt top with the batting and backing is time-consuming. Open the batting several days before you need it and place over a bed or flat on the floor to help flatten the creases caused from its being folded up in the bag for so long.

Iron the backing piece, folding in half both vertically and horizontally and pressing to mark centers.

If you will not be quilting on a frame, place the backing right side down on a clean floor or table. Start in the center and push any wrinkles or bunches flat. Use masking tape to tape the edges to the floor or large clips to hold the backing to the edges of the table. The backing should be taut.

Place the batting on top of the backing, matching centers using fold lines as guides; flatten out any wrinkles. Trim the batting to the same size as the backing.

Fold the quilt top in half lengthwise and place on top of the batting, wrong side against the batting, matching centers. Unfold quilt and, working from the center to the outside edges, smooth out any wrinkles or lumps.

To hold the quilt layers together for quilting, baste by hand or use safety pins. If basting by hand, thread a long thin needle with a long piece of unknotted white or off-white thread. Starting in the center and leaving a long tail, make 4"–6" stitches toward the outside edge of the quilt top, smoothing as you baste. Start at the center again and work toward the outside as shown in Figure 6.

Figure 6
Baste from the center
to the outside edges.

If quilting by machine, you may prefer to use safety pins for holding your quilt sandwich together. Start in the center of the quilt and pin to the outside, leaving pins open until all are placed. When you are satisfied that all layers are smooth, close the pins.

Quilting

Hand Quilting. Hand quilting is the process of placing stitches through the quilt top, batting and backing to hold them together. While it is a functional process, it also adds beauty and loft to the finished quilt.

To begin, thread a sharp between needle with an 18" piece of quilting thread. Tie a small knot in the end of the thread. Position the needle about 1/2" to 1" away from the starting point on quilt top. Sink the needle through the top into the batting layer but not through the backing. Pull the needle up at the starting point of the quilting design. Pull the needle and thread until the knot sinks through the top into the batting (Figure 7).

Figure 7
Start the needle through the top layer of fabric 1/2"–1" away from quilting line with knot on top of the fabric.

Tips & Techniques

Knots should not show on the quilt top or back. Learn to sink the knot into the batting at the beginning and ending of the quilting thread for successful stitches.

When you have nearly run out of thread, wind the thread around the needle several times to make a small knot and pull it close to the fabric. Insert the needle into the fabric on the quilting line and come out with the needle 1/2" to 1" away, pulling the knot into the fabric layers the same as when you started. Pull and cut thread close to fabric. The end should disappear inside after cutting. Some quilters prefer to take a backstitch with a loop through it for a knot to end.

Making 12–18 stitches per inch is a nice goal, but a more realistic goal is seven to nine stitches per inch. If you cannot accomplish this right away, strive for even stitches—all the same size—that look as good on the back as on the front.

Tips & Techniques

Use a thimble to prevent sore fingers when hand quilting. The finger that is under the quilt to feel the needle as it passes through the backing is the one that is most apt to get sore from the pin pricks. Some quilters purchase leather thimbles for this finger while others try home remedies. One simple aid is masking tape wrapped around the finger. With the tape you will still be able to feel the needle, but it will not prick your skin. Over time calluses build up and these fingers get toughened up, but with every vacation from quilting, they will become soft and the process begins again.

Some stitchers like to take a backstitch at the beginning while others prefer to begin the first stitch here. Take small, even running stitches along the marked quilting line (Figure 8). Keep one hand positioned underneath to feel the needle go all the way through to the backing.

Figure 8
Make small, even running stitches on marked quilting line.

End of sidebars

Machine Quilting. Successful machine quilting requires practice and a good relationship with your sewing machine.

Prepare the quilt for machine quilting in the same way as for hand quilting. Use safety pins to hold the layers together instead of basting with thread.

Presser-foot quilting is best used for straight-line quilting because the presser bar lever does not need to be continually lifted.

Set the machine on a longer stitch length (3 or eight to 10 stitches to the inch). Too tight a stitch causes puckering and fabric tucks, either on the quilt top or backing. An even-feed or walking foot helps to eliminate the tucks and puckering by feeding the upper and lower layers through the machine evenly. Before you begin, loosen the amount of pressure on the presser foot.

Special machine-quilting needles work best to penetrate the three layers in your quilt.

Decide on a design. Quilting in the ditch is not quite as visible, but if you quilt with the feed dogs engaged, it means turning the quilt frequently. It is not easy to fit a rolled-up quilt through the small opening on the sewing machine head.

Meander quilting is the easiest way to machine-quilt—and it is fun. Meander quilting is done using an appliqué or darning foot with the feed dogs dropped. It is sort of like scribbling. Simply move the quilt top around under the foot and make stitches in a random pattern to fill the space. The same method may be used to outline a quilt design. The trick is the same as in hand quilting; you are striving for stitches of uniform size. Your hands are in complete control of the design.

If machine quilting is of interest to you, there are several very good books available at quilt shops that will help you become a successful machine quilter.

Tied Quilts or Comforters. Would you rather tie your quilt layers together than quilt them? Tied quilts are often referred to as comforters. The advantage of tying is that it takes so much less time and the required skills can be learned quickly.

If a top will be tied, choose a thick, bonded batting—one that will not separate during washing. For tying, use pearl cotton, embroidery floss or strong yarn in colors that match or coordinate with the fabrics in your quilt top.

Decide on a pattern for tying. Many quilts are tied at the corners and centers of the blocks and at sashing joints. Try to tie every 4"–6". Special designs can be used for tying, but most quilts are tied in conventional ways. Begin tying in the center and work to the outside edges.

To make the tie, thread a large needle with a long thread (yarn, floss or crochet cotton); do not knot. Push the needle through the quilt top to the back, leaving a 3"–4" length on top. Move the needle to the next position without cutting thread. Take another stitch through the layers; repeat until thread is almost used up.

Cut thread between stitches, leaving an equal amount of thread on each stitch. Tie a knot with the two thread ends. Tie again to make a square knot referring to Figure 9. Trim thread ends to desired length.

Figure 9
Make a square knot as shown.

Finishing the Edges

After your quilt is tied or quilted, the edges need to be finished. Decide how you want the edges of your quilt finished before layering the backing and batting with the quilt top.

Without Binding—Self-Finish. There is one way to eliminate adding an edge finish. This is done before quilting. Place the batting on a flat surface. Place the pieced top right side up on the batting. Place the backing right sides together with the pieced top. Pin and/or baste the layers together to hold flat referring to page 171.

Begin stitching in the center of one side using a 1/4" seam allowance, reversing at the beginning and end of the seam. Continue stitching all around and back to the beginning side. Leave a 12" or larger opening. Clip corners to reduce excess. Turn right side out through the opening; slipstitch the opening closed by hand. The quilt may now be quilted by hand or machine.

The disadvantage to this method is that once the edges are sewn in, any creases or wrinkles that might form during the quilting process cannot be flattened out. Tying is the preferred method for finishing a quilt constructed using this method.

Bringing the backing fabric to the front is another way to finish the quilt's edge without binding. To accomplish this, complete the quilt as for hand or machine quilting. Trim the batting *only* even with the front. Trim the backing 1" larger than the completed top all around.

Turn the backing edge in 1/2" and then turn over to the front along edge of batting. The folded edge may be machine-stitched close to the edge through all layers, or blind-stitched in place to finish.

The front may be turned to the back. If using this method, a wider front border is needed. The backing and batting are trimmed 1" *smaller* than the top and the top edge is turned under 1/2" and then turned to the back and stitched in place.

One more method of self-finish may be used. The top and backing may be stitched together by hand at the edge. To accomplish this, all quilting must be stopped 1/2" from the quilt-top edge. The top and backing of the quilt are trimmed even and the batting is trimmed to 1/4"–1/2" smaller. The edges of the top and backing are turned in 1/4"–1/2" and blind-stitched together at the very edge.

These methods do not require the use of extra fabric and save time in preparation of binding strips; they are not as durable as an added binding.

Binding. The technique of adding extra fabric at the edges of the quilt is called binding. The binding encloses the edges and adds an extra layer of fabric for durability.

To prepare the quilt for the addition of the binding, trim the batting and backing layers flush with the top of the quilt using a rotary cutter and ruler or shears. Using a walking-foot attachment (sometimes called an even-feed foot attachment), machine-baste the three layers together all around approximately 1/8" from the cut edge.

The list of materials given with each quilt in this book often includes a number of yards of self-made or purchased binding. Bias binding may be purchased in packages and in many colors. The advantage to self-made binding is that you can use fabrics from your quilt to coordinate colors.

Double-fold, straight-grain binding and double-fold, bias-grain binding are two of the most commonly used types of binding.

Double-fold, straight-grain binding is used on smaller projects with right-angle corners. Double-fold, bias-grain binding is best suited for bed-size quilts or quilts with rounded corners.

To make double-fold, straight-grain binding, cut 2 1/4"-wide strips of fabric across the width or down the length of the fabric totaling the perimeter of the quilt plus 10". Join strips as shown in Figure 10; press in half wrong sides together along the length using an iron on the cotton setting with *no* steam.

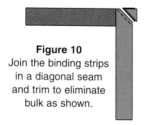

Figure 10
Join the binding strips in a diagonal seam and trim to eliminate bulk as shown.

Lining up the raw edges, place the binding on the top of the quilt and begin sewing (again using the walking foot) approximately 6" from the beginning of the binding strip. Stop sewing 1/4" from the first corner, leave the needle in the quilt, turn and sew diagonally to the corner as shown in Figure 11.

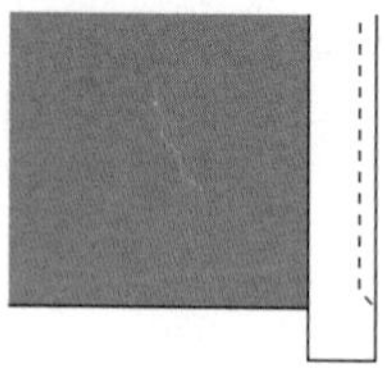

Figure 11
Sew to within 1/4" of corner; leave needle in quilt, turn and stitch diagonally off the corner of the quilt.

Fold the binding at a 45-degree angle up and away from the quilt as shown in Figure 12 and back down flush with the raw edges. Starting at the top raw edge of the quilt, begin sewing the next side as shown in Figure 13. Repeat at the next three corners.

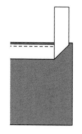 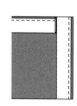

Figure 12
Fold binding at a 45-degree angle up and away from quilt.

Figure 13
Fold the binding strips back down, flush with the raw edge, and begin sewing.

As you approach the beginning of the binding strip, stop stitching and overlap the binding 1/2" from the edge; trim. Join the two ends with a 1/4" seam allowance and press the seam open. Reposition the joined binding along the edge of the quilt and resume stitching to the beginning.

To finish, bring the folded edge of the binding over the raw edges and blind-stitch the binding in place over the machine-stitching line on the backside. Hand-miter the corners on the back as shown in Figure 14.

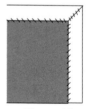

Figure 14
Miter and stitch the corners as shown.

If you are making a quilt to be used on a bed, you will want to use double-fold, bias-grain bindings because the many threads that cross each other along the fold at the edge of the quilt make it a more durable binding.

Cut 2 1/4"-wide bias strips from a large square of fabric. Join the strips as illustrated in Figure 10 and press the seams open. Cut the beginning end of the bias strip at a 45-degree angle; fold the angled raw edge under 1/4" and press. Fold the joined strips in half along the length, wrong sides together, and press with *no* steam (Figure 15).

Figure 15
Fold end in and press strip in half.

Follow the same procedures as previously described for preparing the quilt top and sewing the binding to the quilt top. Treat the corners just as you treated them with straight-grain binding.

Since you are using bias-grain binding, you do have the option to just eliminate the corners if this option doesn't interfere with the patchwork in the quilt. To round the corners, place a your dinner plates at the corner and rotary-cut the gentle curve (Figure 16).

Figure 16
Round corners to eliminate
square-corner finishes.

As you approach the beginning of the binding strip, stop stitching and lay the end across the beginning so it will slip inside the fold. Cut the end at a 45-degree angle so the raw edges are contained inside the beginning of the strip (Figure 17); resume stitching to the beginning. Bring the fold to the back of the quilt and hand-stitch as previously described.

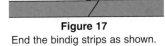

Figure 17
End the bindig strips as shown.

Overlapped corners are not quite as easy as rounded ones, but a bit easier than mitering. To make overlapped corners, sew binding strips to opposite sides of the quilt top. Stitch edges down to finish. Trim ends even.

Sew a strip to each remaining side, leaving 1 1/2"–2" excess at each end. Turn quilt over and fold end in even with previous finished edge as shown in Figure 18.

Fold binding in toward quilt and stitch down as before, enclosing the previous bound edge in the seam as shown in Figure 19. It may be necessary to trim the folded-down section to reduce bulk.

Making Continuous Bias Binding

Instead of cutting individual bias strips and sewing them together, you may make continuous bias binding.

Cut a square 21" x 21" from chosen binding fabric. Cut the square once on the diagonal to make two triangles as shown in Figure 20. With right sides together, join the two triangles with a 1/4" seam allowance as shown in Figure 21; press seam open to reduce bulk.

Figure 20
Cut 21" square on
the diagonal.

Figure 21
Sew the triangles
together.

Mark lines every 2 1/4" on the wrong side of the fabric as shown in Figure 22. Bring the short ends together, right sides together, offsetting one line as shown in Figure 31; stitch to make a tube. This will seam awkward.

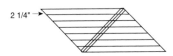

Figure 22
Mark lines 2 1/4" apart on wrong side.

Begin cutting at point A as shown in Figure 24; continue cutting along marked line to make one continuous strip. Fold strip in half along length with wrong sides together; press. Sew to quilt edges as instructed previously for bias binding.

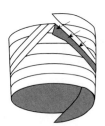

Figure 23
Sew short ends together,
offsetting lines to make a tube.

Figure 24
Cut along marked lines,
starting at A.

Final Touches

If your quilt will be hung on the wall, a hanging sleeve is required. Other options include purchased plastic rings or fabric tabs. The best choice is a fabric sleeve, which will evenly distribute the weight of the quilt across the top edge, rather than at selected spots where tabs or rings are stitched, and will keep the quilt hanging straight and not damage the batting.

To make a sleeve, measure across the top of the finished quilt. Cut an 8"-wide piece of muslin equal to that length—you may need to seam several muslin strips together to make the required length.

Fold in 1/4" on each end of the muslin strip and press. Fold again and stitch to hold. Fold the muslin strip lengthwise with right sides together; sew along the long side to make a tube. Turn the tube right side out; press with seam at bottom or centered on the back.

Hand-stitch the tube along the top of the quilt and the bottom of the tube to the quilt back making sure the quilt lies flat. Stitches should not go through to the front of the quilt and don't need to be too close together as shown in Figure 25.

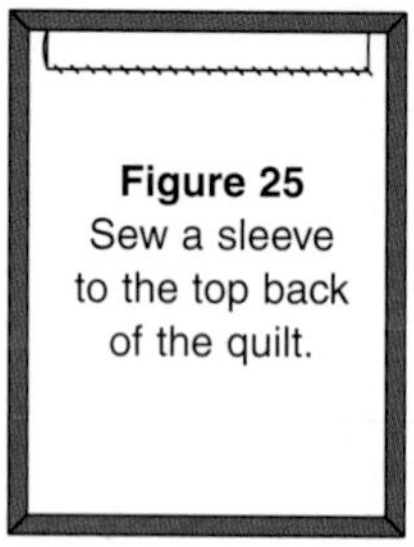

Figure 25
Sew a sleeve to the top back of the quilt.

Slip a wooden dowel or long curtain rod through the sleeve to hang.

When the quilt is finally complete, it should be signed and dated. Use a permanent pen on the back of the quilt. Other methods include cross-stitching your name and date on the front or back or making a permanent label that may be stitched to the back. ❖

Special Thanks

We would like to thamk the talented quilt designers whose work is featured in this collection.

Leslie Beck
Posy Silhouettes, ...162
Barbara Clayton
Nativity Wall Quilt, ...35
Blue Floral Lap Quilt, ...66
Gather Ye Roses, ...130
Holly Daniels
By the Seashore, ...60
Sue Harvey
Teddy-Go-Round, ...8
Celebration Quilt, ...23
Flaky Friends, ...50
Posey Patch, ...106
Pretty Maids Quilt, ...116
Sandra Hatch
Checkerboard Four-Patch, ...32
Hearts Afloat, ...63

Pearl Louise Krush
Teddy Bear Quilt & Tote, ...18
Hearts United,.................................93
Ruched Roses & Baskets, ...112
Flowers & Grapes Baskets, ...119
Kate Laucomer
Happy Penguins,.............................15
Stars & Stripes Table Quilt,.............96
Flower Basket Mantel Cover, ...155
Chris Malone
Christmas Keepsake Stocking, ...54
The Earth Laughs in Flowers,........123
Connie Rand
Dragonfly Meadow, ...90
Judith Sandstrom
Baby Blocks With Love, ...27
Christine Schultz
Oriental Garden, ...150

Marian Shenk
Sleepy Baby Buggy, ...11
Golden Pansies Table Mat, ...74
Petals & Leaves Pillow, ...136
Spring Bouquets, ...142
Flowers at the Crossroads,............165
Willow Ann Sirch
Christmas Cardinal, ...40
Blue for You Kimono,........................78
Maple Leaf Ragtime,......................103
Julie Weaver
Sign of the Season, ...46
Sunny Days, ...71
Evergreen Lane, ...86
United We Stand, ...100
Homespun Pumpkin Patch Vest, ..159

Fabrics & Supplies

Page 8: *Teddy-Go-Round* —Perfect Cotton Just Like Wool batting and Mettler Silk-Finish thread and Poly-Sheen machine-embroidery thread from American & Efird. Machine-quilted by Brenda Cookson.
Page 23: *Celebration*—Basics and Aqua Textures Wave fabric collections from Northcott, Hobbs Heirloom Organic Bleached Cotton batting and Mettler Silk-Finish thread from American & Efird. The sample was machine-pieced by Emma Jean Cook on a Brother PQ-1500 and machine-quilted by Brenda Cookson.
Page 27: *Baby Blocks with Love*—Fabrics from Springs Industries, Hobbs Heirloom 100-percent cotton batting and DMC quilting thread.

Page 50: *Flaky Friends*—Hobbs Heirloom Organic Cotton Batting, 505 Spray and Fix basting spray, Mettler Silk-Finish thread and Signature machine-quilting thread from American & Efird and Theresa's Hand Dyed Buttons from Hillcreek Designs.
Page 54: *Christmas Keepsake Stocking*—Kreinik No. 8 gold metallic fine braid.
Page 76: *Blue for You Kimono*—Bali fabrics.
Page 90: *Dragonfly Meadow*— Hatfields fabric collection from Tenderberry Stitches by Sharon Reynolds from Northcott/Monarch and Hobbs Heirloom cotton batting with scrim binder.

Page 106: *Pretty Maids*— Charleston fabric collection from Northcott, Hobbs Heirloom Organic Cotton batting and Metter Silk-Finish thread from American & Efird. Stitched by Emma Jean Cook on a Brother Nouvelle PQ-1500 and machine-quilted by Sandy Boobar.
Page 116: *Posy Patch*—Perfect Cotton White batting, 505 Spray and Fix basting spray, Brandy's Master Yo-Yo Template and Mettler Silk-Finish thread and Signature machine-quilting thread from American & Efird. Machine-stitched by Emma Jean Cook on a Brother Nouvelle PQ 1500 and machine-quilted by Brenda Cookson.